painting
the Walls red

the Uninhibited
Woman's Guide
to a Fabulous Life After 40

Judy Ford, author of
Single: The Art of Being Satisfied, Fulfilled, and Independent

Adams Media
Avon, Massachusetts

Published by
Adams Media, an F+W Publications Company
57 Littlefield Street, Avon, MA 02322. U.S.A.
www.adamsmedia.com

ISBN: 1-59337-384-8

Printed in Canada.

J I H G F E D C B A

Library of Congress Cataloging-in-Publication Data
Ford, Judy
Painting the walls red / Judy Ford.
p.   cm.
ISBN 1-59337-384-8
1. Middle aged women—Psychology. 2. Middle aged women—
Attitudes. 3. Aging—Psychological aspects. 4. Self-actualization
(Psychology) in middle age. 5. Middle aged women—Life skill guides. I. Title.

HQ1059.4.F67 2005
305.244'2—dc22
                                    2005005214

This book is available at quantity discounts for bulk purchases.
For information, please call 1-800-872-5627.

Contents

"There is also in each of us the maverick, the darling stubborn one who won't listen, who insists, who chooses preference or the spirited guess over yardsticks or even history. I suspect this maverick is somewhat what the soul is, or at least that the soul lives close by."

—MARY OLIVER

To women everywhere
who open their hearts and
paint the world
in sunshine.

Acknowledgments

I am jumping up and down with happiness and gratitude to the women who generously shared with me their missteps, victories, opinions, and inside secrets for creating fabulous life after forty:

Gethen Bassett, Patricia Bragg, Cindy Bittenfield, Barbara Deede, Vedika Dietrich, Lee Dhyanam, Surya Gardener, Leanne Goulding, Marla Greenway, Marie Guise, Janet Habereush, Regina Hansen, Marjie Hartvigson, Andrea Hurst, Anne Lise Finnbraaten, Antonia Kabalov, Ann Killian, Virgina Kimball, Aletha Lundblad, Melissa Mager, Fryma Mantel, Ragini Michaels, Pat Minkove, Cynthia Muszynski, Chloe Patton, Cat Saunders, Cathy Schalkle, Phyllis Sorensen, Jean Theisen, and Ann Williamson.

Thumbs-up to the wise men who know the value of a woman with experience: Jay Schlechter, Ph.D., Edward Vasder, and Daryl Deede.

Bouquets of appreciation to Danielle Chiotti, my receptive and responsive editor; to literary agent Jenny Bent; to copyeditor Christina Schoen; and to Beth Gissinger and Meredith D. O'Hayre for spreading the news of my books around town. Without these creative people, this book would not be.

May I Introduce You?

How can you describe a woman? Just when you think you know what makes her tick, she changes, tries on a new aspect of herself, or accentuates her other side. That's what makes each of us so special, so unique, and so outrageously poetic. We refuse to fit into a box, and even if we were willing, there isn't a box pliable or large enough to hold our spirit. We become more fabulous every year.

Women in the second half of life are incredible, and I intend to spread the word. We do not accept the myth that youthful beauty is the only beauty. We do not accept the myth that our lives are over because we are over thirty. We refuse to be trapped by stereotypes. The midlife truth is that women of a certain age are funny, tender, and fully alive.

While writing this book, I developed a huge appreciation for our femininity, our creativity, and our spirit. I have gotten to know all the wise, kooky, creative women in this book through my interviews with them. They inspire me, not because they are rich, perfect, or have it all together, but because they are refreshingly honest. Honest about who they are, what they have been through, what they know is true, and what they are still struggling to figure out. They are willing to share their heartaches, cry over their losses, laugh about their own foibles until tears roll down their pink and mellowing cheeks. They never give up. They will roll up their sleeves and pull themselves out of the muck by their comfy shoe straps if they have to. These women are shining stars, not in a "look-at-me-I'm-a-celebrity" way, but rather with an "anything-is-possible" attitude. These women are the sugar, spice, and salt of the earth. They lift me up.

Let me introduce you to them. Each one is an artist—and maybe not in the way you think. They are artists in the fine and messy art of living. They are experts at figuring out what is needed. They are embracing the midyears with imagination and elbow grease. They plant gardens and wipe noses. They can open a can of soup or cook from scratch. They paint everything—walls, canvas, fingernails. They dance, but not always in rhythm. They sing, but not necessarily in tune. They know where they are lacking, and they either cheerfully accept their quirks or move heaven and earth to change and grow better. They definitely are not lazy, unless of course they feel like being lazy, then they will happily lounge around until they are good and ready to get up and start over. These women have been through it all—cramps and heavy-duty winged-sided maxi pads, sleepless nights and panty liners. They have taken abuse, dished out advice, and forgotten what they went into the next room for. Their hearts have grown big enough to forgive you and set you straight in the process. They have been on their knees, they have cried their hearts out, and they have kept going for the sake of humankind. They have sacrificed and still they rejoice in the smallest of blessings. Their lives are their prayer, their song, and their dance. They fill their homes with laughter. They are living art forms, walking testimonies that age does not define a woman. Women in the second half of life are finding their place, making their peace, and discovering that there are more dreams to achieve. This book is a celebration of women who know that age does not limit who they are or who they might become. Age is an attitude and these women are on fire; they know what needs to be done and they are delighted to do it.

The lessons in this book are true and the facts as accurate as the woman telling the story remembers. Many of the women have used their real names and others have chosen a playful pseudonym. Not because they have anything to hide, but because it's more fun this way. Besides, when you are a juicy artist, you can change your name to match your dress, your mood, and who you are becoming. These women do not take themselves as seriously as they did when they thought they would live forever. They have reached the age of knowing that they are closer to the end of their life than to the beginning, and that realization softens them and turns them more passionately playful than ever.

You are an artist, too. If I knew you or if there were more pages in this book, I'm certain I'd want to tell your story. I intend to spread the word about women in the second half of life. I want to change the silly perception that we are all outdated. I want to inspire young women by our example. We know that even when life is so difficult that we don't think we can go on, it is still absolutely wonderful. We know that women all over the world get up every morning—with aches and pains—and do the impossible. Here's to you and women everywhere, the women who do the impossible!

Section One...

The Inside Scoop

MIDDLESCENCE

Brace yourself. Here is the inside scoop: Somewhere between forty and sixty, you are going to feel and act like a teenager again. We've been through adolescence, our roaring twenties, and whirling thirties. Then comes middlescence. Just when we thought we were grown and settled—wham! Our hormones are rearranging themselves. Again. We are irrational. Again. We are tempted. Again. We are needy. Again. We are moody. Again. Dramatic. Again. Depressed. Again. Restless. Again. And we are excited.

Welcome to Messy Middlescence

I am grown up!

I am older!

I am middle-aged!

I knew it was true, but it didn't sink in until I attended my twenty-fifth high school reunion. When I put on the name tag and walked into the banquet room and saw 127 salt-and-pepper-haired strangers standing around in a daze, that was my moment of reckoning. It was like being hit in the stomach. "Am I in the wrong room?" I wondered. "Surely I don't belong here. Do I look *thaaat* bad?" Couldn't possibly, I reassured myself. I am the exception.

Then I bumped into him. My high school sweetheart. The guy I lusted after, lost sleep over, and cried over. The curly-haired hunk that I made out with under the bleachers. The star quarterback, the hard body, the guy that I once fantasized about marrying. The one I broke up with when I went away to college, the one I lost track of, the one I think about when life gets dull. When we finally had a moment together, he said, "Judy, is that really you? You look good." "You look good," he repeated. How many times can a person hear "You look good" before getting suspicious? My high school sweetheart had a paunch that looked like he had swallowed the football that he used to score touchdowns with. That was my clue. I could no longer stay in denial. I had crossed over and I couldn't go back. The middle-aged goose was out of the bottle.

I knew that middle age was coming, but I did not expect it to come so quickly. I cannot remember exactly when I crossed over the invisible line, but I did. Crossing over from young and hip to middle aged and not so hip is very disconcerting. When I realized that I was forty-something and not still twentysomething, I was thunderstruck. I was not prepared for the jolt. None of us are prepared. How could we prepare for such a rude awakening? Oh sure, I had celebrated my fortieth birthday, but I did not come to grips with the harsh reality of being in the middle until I attended that reunion.

A reunion with a gaggle of middle-aged geese is astonishing, but equally shocking is the realization that there is a phase of life called "middlescence" and that you're right in the middle of it. Middlescence is messy. I did not expect messes. I thought I'd left messiness behind. No one told me that I would not necessarily act, think, or feel grown up. When you're a kid, you think that grownups have all the answers. As a grownup, I have some answers, but I do not have them all. When you're a kid, you think anyone over forty is finished. I am not finished. When you're a kid, you think that adults are boring. I am not boring. When you're a kid, you think that grownups are almost dead. I am not dead yet.

Contrary to popular belief, the middle years are not static. They are full of adjustments. I change, rearrange, shift, fall in and out of love, change directions, fall apart, pick up the pieces, settle down, and re-evaluate. Middlescence is one mysterious surprise followed by another. Just when I got used to being a mother, my daughter grew up and moved out. Just when I thought I was stable and secure, something shifted and I found myself plopped in the middle of some grand fine-tuning. Just when I was feeling content because my best friend Jean had moved close by, she and her husband sold their home again and moved away. Life is ever-changing and I'm learning about graceful transitions. I am figuring out that when something goes wrong, it does not mean that there is something wrong with me.

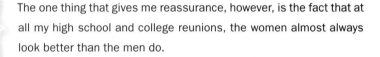

The one thing that gives me reassurance, however, is the fact that at all my high school and college reunions, the women almost always look better than the men do.

Middle age is a benchmark. I feel alone and not quite like myself. I ask myself, "What is it all about?" I earnestly, passionately attempt to figure that out. I have big questions. I search everywhere for meaning and purpose. I seek joy. I am on a mysterious quest to uncover the why of the why. I do not always know which way to look. The one thing that gives me reassurance, however, is the fact that at all my high school and college reunions, the women almost always look better than the men do.

To Do or Not to Do

1. Prepare for reunions at least a year in advance. Figure out what image you want to present and work diligently on it.

2. Look up your high school sweetheart before the reunion. That way you will recognize him when he says hello.

3. When you enter middlescence, read the opening lines of Dante's *Divine Comedy* or Elizabeth Buchan's *Revenge of the Middle-Aged Woman*.

4. If you feel like you are going crazy once you enter middlescence, don't! No need to check yourself in to a psychiatric ward or put on a straitjacket. Confusion is normal for midlifers.

5. Search for the why of the why. No matter what, remind yourself that the second half of life is flavored with big, big questions.

"If you have ever been called defiant, incorrigible, forward, cunning, insurgent, unruly, rebellious, you're on the right track."

—DR. CLARISSA PINKOLA ESTÉS

"It's Hot in Here" Shuffle

You can't predict hot flashes. They come when they want to, and they have their own rhythm.

In the middle of January, the coldest month in Maine, Sally was greeted by her first hot flash. Nick, her husband, was driving and Rebecca, their sixteen-year-old daughter, was in the back seat. They were on the way to a mountain cabin for a weekend in the snow. Sally was enjoying the scenery when, without warning, a blush of warmth enveloped her shoulders. The heat crept onto her neck, up to her chin, and over her face. In less than a minute, she had gone from comfortable to warm to hot and sweating.

Suddenly, in what seemed like one perfectly choreographed move, Sally pulled off her sweater, rolled down the window, twisted her body parallel to the passenger window, and stuck her entire head, neck, and shoulders into the fresh, cold Maine air. The entire maneuver took less than thirty seconds, quicker than either her husband or daughter could ask, "What are you doing?" By the time they gathered their wits together enough to inquire what was going on, she was sitting straight in her seat and rolling the window back up. You can't predict hot flashes. They come when they want to, and they have their own rhythm.

Melanie falls into bed exhausted. She tosses and turns, getting up to pee three or four times, and in the morning her joints wake up aching. She drags her bones out of bed and they snap, crackle, and pop. She wears super Tampax and winged-sided pads at the same time because her monthly flow is not monthly anymore—it's heavy and irregular. She gets hot when everyone else is cold. She goes to handfuls of doctors, and they diagnose a plethora of ailments. "It could be chronic fatigue, depression, low thyroid, autoimmune, tooth decay, allergies, or stress." They suggest a cure: "Take two antidepressants and come back next year." At forty-three, Melanie knows her body well enough to know that her symptoms are not just her imagination. She is determined to find answers and take responsibility for her own health care. She changes doctors three times until she settles on a woman internist with a holistic perspective.

Leesa and her girlfriends are having similar symptoms. They compare aches and pains and swap natural remedies. When Leesa hears a woman doctor talking about her exact symptoms—headaches, mood swings, and heavy flow—on the health segment of the early morning news, she calls her older sister Heather. Together the two of them figure it out. Leesa isn't crazy after all—she is merely perimenopausal. So is Sally with her hot flashes and Melanie with her aching joints and exhaustion. Perimenopause is the medical jargon for the hormonal swings before the last period. Estrogen is tenacious, and it can take years before that hormone finally settles down.

To put it simply, your perimenopausal symptoms are caused by your hormones rearranging themselves. "It's hot in here" is more than a hot flash—it's the declaration of a woman on a mission. She is hot and she is making herself comfortable. She is taking charge. She is way beyond suffering in silence. She will turn the heat down in the middle of winter and open the windows if she needs to. She will talk with friends and coworkers, compare symptoms, and discuss treatment options. She will search for a compatible professional. She will change doctors if she doesn't get good answers or proper attention. She is educating herself about her body and hormones.

We are more than hot flashes, more than bodily functions.

Welcome to the change of life, as some call it. I personally prefer to think that women evolve. All the women I know are evolving. We are more than hot flashes, more than bodily functions. It takes awareness and spunk to understand and take charge of what's happening. The first hot flash is like the first menstrual cramp—it sneaks up, it's uncomfortable, and it grabs our attention. At first we're not sure what it is. It takes discernment to identify pesky hot flashes. "Is it just me or is it hot in here?" we ask, and when we hear "It's you" for the umpteenth time, we are finally able to recognize what's happening. Some people, including some medical professionals, insist that menopause doesn't begin until fifty, but just ask any woman who's gone through it and she'll tell you that's not true. Hot flashes are as personal and as varied as cramps. They can start in our thirties and come every hour. Or they may not start until our forties or fifties. Flushed cheeks are not just figments of imagination. If we are hot, we are hot, and that's the truth.

To Do or Not to Do

1. If someone hints, "You're going through the change," correct them instantly. Tell them, "I'm evolving."
2. Adopt this mantra: "If you're hot, you're hot."
3. If your doctor prescribes antidepressants and you're not depressed, change doctors.
4. Do the midnight shuffle. Turn down the heat, open the windows, let in the fresh air, pee, and get back in bed.
5. Talk about your symptoms to women who have been there. They won't for even one minute think you are crazy.

"Perimenopause is simply the years before menopause. Menopause is that one day event when you get your very last period. Pretty simple, huh?"

—Nisha Jackson, Ph.D.

Dropping, Drooping, Hanging Down

Unaware of any major modifications, forty-seven-year-old Gracie steps into the shower, glances down at her nude body—the body she's known for more than four decades—and there's the evidence. Two or three gray pubic hairs pushing out from the rest. Proof that her girlhood is fading and a newfangled body is forming.

Middle age is ludicrous. There are so many minute changes, small transitions, and tiny losses that it's hard to keep track of what's happening. Eyelids dropping, skin sagging, gravity systematically pulling us down. Midlife is like puberty. Our body is altered in so many ways, and when the metamorphosis begins it's confusing.

Gracie stands in front of the mirror, shaking. Her mother didn't tell her, her girlfriends didn't warn her. "Pubic hair turns gray?" she shouts. That she didn't expect! What can be done about that? She finds satisfaction in taking good care of her body, in eating well, and in going to the gym. She is pleased that she can pass for thirty, but pubic hair, she had not considered pubic hair. She whitens her teeth, creams her face, strengthens her muscles, and flexes her joints. Still, there are some body parts you shouldn't mess with. "Like laugh lines," she says. "I've got permanent laugh lines and I'm not laughing." OK, so it's not tragic, but in a society that celebrates youth and disregards the wisdom of its elders, sagging skin and descending boobs come as a quite a blow. No wonder we're raging. "I'm getting older," she sighs, "but it's not all bad." Yet she still misses the freshness of youth. Coming to terms with the fact that our once perky breasts are closer to our waist than to our shoulders requires a new set of survival skills. It often seems as if our femininity is under attack, as if our body is betraying us. It is disorienting, and, like Gracie, we miss the firm bounce of youth.

> Coming to terms with the fact that our once perky breasts are closer to our waist than to our shoulders requires a new set of survival skills.

"Physical beauty counts much more for women than it does for men," says forty-nine-year-old Mary. "For women in our society beauty is associated with being young, so I'm feeling anxious about looking older." To deal with her unsettled feelings, she searches for new reference points. "I look at women in their fifties and beyond," she says, "and I can sense who's comfortable with their age and that's encouraging to me."

Our self-esteem was never completely tied up with our looks, but it's harder to love our chin when it's doubling. True, we weren't always happy when we were young; in fact, there were plenty of times when we were miserable and full of self-doubt. Fortunately, middle age brings a contentedness, an optimism, and an urge to stay vital. Yes, we may be dropping, drooping, and sagging, but that is not the only thing that is happening. We are gaining self-respect, renewing our energy, and finding our creative power. We are discovering that life is good and it's good to be in the thick of it. "Every time I say something negative about my looks," Mary says, "I counter it by appreciating two other things. If I say, 'Yuck, look at those crow's-feet,' I make a rebuttal and say, 'I've got feet and I'm going places.' "

If we constantly criticize ourselves and fail to appreciate our beautiful bodies, we will shrink from living. If we only look backward at our youth, we become unable to see how lovely we really are. If we are willing to accept and approve of ourselves, we find joy in being alive and we are able to go through middlescence full tilt, with our heads and hearts high. "Hey, I'm happening," Mary says. "It's just that my wrapping is getting a little wrinkled and messy so people don't immediately see the real me inside. You may call it delusional, but it works for me."

To Do or Not to Do

1. Have a midlife body appreciation fest with your girlfriends. Remind each other that we are beautiful no matter how our bodies are softening.
2. Get it out of your system—order a martini and pout about what is drooping.
3. When you see a woman who is comfortable with her age and herself, give her the thumbs up.
4. Name three women (not movie stars) who are aging with savoir-faire and grace.

5. Tell jokes and cheer each other up! Laughing about drooping boobs and eyelids is more invigorating than endlessly comparing ourselves to youthful boobs and eyelids.

"Things are going to get a lot worse before they get worse."

—LILY TOMLIN

Midlife Funk and Creative Soup

First of all, I want to reassure you that a midlife funk is normal, natural, and healthy and can lead to something grand. Midlife funk is an adult developmental stage similar in some ways to what we went through in adolescence. At midlife, our psyches are rearranging, we are switching from mundane tasks to the call of our soul. Midlife funk is that jumping-off point where we go from following our heads to following our hearts. We are hearing the call of our creative, authentic, and spiritual selves.

You know you are in a midlife funk when:

1. You are restless, bored, lonely, and slightly anxious, but you can't pin it on anything in particular.
2. You are beginning to notice and count wrinkles.
3. The kids are either getting ready to move out, already have, or you are thinking about having another baby.
4. You have come to the rude awakening that your life has not turned out as you had planned.
5. You are sentimental and wonder where the good old days have gone.
6. Your daughter wants to update your hair and wardrobe.

7. You are happily married, but you feel as if he doesn't really know you.

8. You are happily unmarried and wondering if you made a mistake by divorcing your ex, whom you haven't seen in a few years.

9. The older you get the less you know for sure, and you're wondering "what's it all about."

10. You aren't getting the bang out of your career that you once did.

Like all transitions, there is a phase of missing what was. We are sentimental. We liked our life, and now it is in flux. We are evolving. Free-floating anxiety, like a dark cloud, hovers over us. We want to escape. We do not know what lies ahead; we are out of sorts and fearful. Like soup simmering on the stove, taking hours to turn flavorful and tasty, we are simmering in the funk. It takes brewing time for middle-aged funk to turn sweet. To view ourselves in a fresh way, to see the possibilities, and to discover what brings meaning and joy takes our active participation. We have to prepare. Something in us is bubbling. Blessings are percolating. We are becoming all that we are destined to be. It is exhilarating.

Within each of us is the "universal urge to create." We have a deep desire to make a contribution to the world, to give birth to something positive, to sprinkle hope on hopelessness. At our center we are incredibly optimistic. At midlife, we are going through a spiritual makeover. Up until now, we've been skimming the surface of our potential. That's the creative soup. A mixture of experiences, desires, dreams, and optimism. It's tapping into trust and faith again. When it comes to play, creativity, enthusiasm, and art, our spirit doesn't need much guidance. Our hearts go pitter-patter.

Creativity is the cure for midlife funk. For every midlife symptom there is a creative remedy. Here are some examples of cures to get you started. Cut fifty strips of paper and store them in a box or a basket. As you discover a creative project that you'd like to do, write the instructions on the strip of paper and put it in the basket. When you're in one of those foggy moods and not thinking clearly, you can go to the creative remedy box and pull out a cure. The cures can be as simple as buying crepe paper, making crepe paper chains, and stringing them around the house. Think about how surprising that will be. Won't that lift you out of the doldrums? A midlife funk treatment can be getting involved in a cause, such as saving the elephants or gorillas. It can be going to film school and making documentaries. Whatever inspires you, go for it. Creativity is our soul's way of making our stamp on the world.

To Do or Not to Do

1. Follow the "universal urge to create." The very first step out of midlife funk is to recognize the creative urge simmering within.
2. Pursue your interests! I'm not suggesting that you take up a hobby merely to take your mind off what is stewing in your psyche. I'm talking about listening to the call of your soul, taking a leap, and going for it.
3. Get sloppy. Make things. Roll around in glitter.
4. Write on stuff. Paint graffiti on the sidewalk.
5. Practice these three soothing words: "I made this." Doesn't that give you the chills?

"It's kind of fun to do the impossible."

—WALT DISNEY

On Becoming a Creative Genius

How did the vision to paint my dining room and living room walls red come to me? And how did I decide that OPI Red, the color of my favorite nail polish, was the perfect red for my rooms? Have you ever had the urge to do something fantastic but stopped yourself before you began? Have you ever been bold and taken a chance? Have you ever wondered where the inspiration came from?

I remember the moment when the intention became clear. I was sitting on the living room floor, my sliding glass door open to let in the cold December air, waiting out a hot flash. In the middle of a hot flash, there's nothing to do but sit down and surrender, wait and allow it to envelope you and pass over. It had taken me a couple of months of trial and error to learn to accept the warmth. No need to wrestle with hot flashes.

Is it the same with inspiration? I let the cold air revive me, and after a space of a few minutes the only remnants of a hot flash were my slightly damp bangs. "There's no need to fend off hot flashes or inspiration," I thought. "Give in, Judy, give in to inspiration."

I was forty-seven and menopausal, and Manda, my daughter, was a teenager. "Mom, you're wasting heat!" she scolded in her impatient, thirteen-year-old tone. "It's freezing in here." Not even her "mom's gone nuts" roll of the eyes dissuaded me from my hot flash or my inspiration . . . "ignore all practical objections" was my mantra at the moment.

What inspires a person? Perhaps it was the reddish pink sunrise that roused me. Perhaps it was one of many rebellious thoughts that I'd been indulging in lately. Maybe it was a twinge of "you only live once," sparked by the Tina Turner CD that I'd been listening to all week. The previous afternoon I'd had a manicure and pedicure. My toes and fingernails were perfectly shaped and painted in my favorite blue-red polish to match my red lipstick. I'm a winter, and red is the ideal accent for me. "That's it," I said out loud. "I'm painting the walls to match my nails."

Whatever it was that moved me, I was quick to respond. I grabbed the Tina Turner CD and bribed Manda with lunch out if she'd ride with me to Home Depot to pick out the paint. "You're going to paint the walls what?" she asked. "OPI Red," I answered. "Cool," she said. I cranked up the volume, "Rolling, rolling, rolling on the river," and within a week the pearly white walls were red and regal. "Ah!" I sighed to Manda, "Isn't freedom grand?"

"Whatever," she said.

"Ah!" I sighed to Manda, "Isn't freedom grand?"
"Whatever," she said.

Manda's nonchalant shrug didn't dampen my midlife verve. The walls looked fantastic. I could sense the rumblings of my unexplored potential. "Hmm," I thought to myself, "Menopause might come with some perks." Why does something as simple as putting color on the wall enliven your spirit? Why is it so important to be creative at this time of life? What are the lessons of midlife? I knew I would be thinking about it.

To Do or Not to Do

1. Pay attention to your hot flashes—they might be the rumblings of untapped genius.
2. Paint one wall to match your favorite nail polish.
3. Paint your nails to match a wall.
4. Don't wrestle with hot flashes. Use them for inspiration.
5. Play Tina Turner CDs. Memorize the words, bounce, and sing along.

Painting the Walls Meditation

Painting can be a meditation, or so my friend Greg, the owner of a decorating paint store, says. He teaches classes on a variety of faux finishes, and he says it is best to paint the walls slowly and with awareness. According to Greg, the secret to a successful painting experience is a good paintbrush and soothing music. He advises me to begin by focusing on the amount of paint on the brush. "Dip the brush into the paint and load the bristles halfway up. Apply spots of paint at a leisurely pace with long, leveling strokes."

I don't paint like that. I paint everything, my hair, under my fingernails, and around my ankles. I use yards of masking tape and old sheets as drop cloths. I like Latin rhythms and a willing helper to entertain me.

Painting the walls can be meditation or celebration; it just depends on your mood at the moment. The perfect color, though, is whatever color you like. What is that? If you do not like the way the walls turn out, you can stop in the middle and start over. The best way to get the job done is to keep your body loose.

"Whim is the plural of women."

—KATHY LETTE

Chronological Fatigue Syndrome

If you sometimes feel absolutely worn out, like a limp wool sweater with frizzy balls, if it takes more energy to do this year what you did twenty years ago, if you feel like screaming, "Leave me alone!", if you are snapping, ragging, or bingeing, then you are definitely suffering from chronological fatigue syndrome. You are doing too much and taking on too much. Crankiness is trying to tell you something. Let's admit it. It's exhausting to be perimenopausal. It takes tremendous effort to keep ourselves from falling apart while painting the walls and looking as good as we do.

You are not crazy, though. You are tired. You need a time-out. There is nothing shameful about needing a break. Just go to your room and shut the door. Remember how well that worked for your children when they were screaming? This is not a marathon. You are painting the walls, not running. You can take a week to finish. You can take a break. You can go to a matinee. You can take a nap in the chair. You can stand in the corner and cry. I highly recommend, however, that you do what I do and take your bed outside.

I moved an antique iron twin bed outside to my deck. It is my secret retreat. That's where I sleep in the summer. On sunny fall days, I pull the folded-up mattress out of the closet, grab pillows and comforters, and take a nap in the chilly air. It's rejuvenating. And it's better than a seaside hideaway because I don't have to pack anything or drive anywhere to get there.

I know what you are thinking: "I've got teenagers to raise"; "I'm at the peak of my career, I can't stop now"; "I have dinner to cook, I have the garden to weed, I've got projects"; "If I don't do it, no one else will." Well, need I remind you that God rested for an entire day? If she can do it, that must mean it's OK. If she can say "no" and take a day off, then that must mean that "no" is an acceptable word. Why do you think a two-year-old spends a whole year learning to say it? Think of it this way, saying "no" when we are tired allows us to say "yes" after we have filled ourselves up again. So many times I have asked a mother or a career woman, "How are you?" and the automatic response is, "I'm exhausted, I'm so tired, I have a million things to do." For once I would love to hear one of them say, "I feel great! I just took a nap, and I'm going home to do art."

Need I remind you that God rested for an entire day? If she can do it, that must mean it's OK.

When a wave of chronological fatigue comes over Jacqui, she goes for a long walk. Walking is her meditation and she's fierce about keeping that retreat for herself. "I don't allow anything to encroach on my walks," she says. Last year she did the Idita-Walk. It's an event in the spirit of the Iditarod Sled Dog Race. The Iditarod Sled Dog Race is 1,049 miles long, from Anchorage to Nome, Alaska. In order to complete an Idita-Walk, you walk thirty minutes for thirty-five days from February 1 through March 21. Jacqui did it and has learned to say "no" because of it: "I said "no" to everything that interfered with my training schedule, and that has taught me to say 'no' when I'm on the verge of exhaustion."

Women are so used to taking care of others and being in charge that we often forget to stop doing and simply be. Someone once said, "We're not human doings, we're human beings." The way I see it is that the first half of life was for doing, the second half of life is more about being. When we don't allow ourselves space and time to listen to the call of our souls, we become deeply fatigued. It's as if our entire body is screaming, "Move out of doing and slide into being." Remember those breathing exercises that you learned when having a baby? Those breathing exercises will come in useful as you slip into being. When someone asks, "What are you doing?" you can answer, "Breathing and being."

To Do or Not to Do

1. Follow God's example. She took the day off. That means it's good for you.
2. Say "no" to doing and "yes" to being.
3. Laze about. Find a slice of sunlight and curl up for however long it takes for you to slow down.
4. If you have to do something, do the Idita-Walk. Complete it and get a T-shirt. Check out *www.idita-walk.com* for more information.
5. Put a happy face sign around your neck that says "The answer is 'no.' "

"As I grow in age, I value older women most of all."

—ANDY ROONEY

So Many Men, So Many Moods

OK girls, it's not just us. Men have hormonal swings and middlescence moods, too. There's even a name for it, andropause. My neighbor Victoria is convinced that male mood swings are much more serious than ours. "We cry and snap a little each month," she says, "but when men get upset, they start a war or rip up the house." She knows firsthand about that. Victoria adores her husband and has benefited from his handyman know-how, but the poor woman must be close to sainthood because she never knows when the remodeling beast will strike. That's because Jake doesn't talk about what's upsetting him— he just rents a jackhammer and tears up the patio. When men get like that, there's no amount of logic or sweet talk that can stop them from tearing walls down or putting walls up. "It's like they've lost their hearing and common sense," Victoria explains. When women are upset all we need in order to calm down is a piece of dark chocolate and a bath. Men can be very unreasonable. Middescence women may be inconsolable at times, but middlescence men are incorrigible.

Jake is notorious for starting a project at the most inconvenient moment, like the time he decided to install crown molding two hours before dinner guests were to arrive. "Why can't you do something helpful, like polish the silver?" Victoria asked him. "Huh?" Jake replied. "We don't need crown molding right now!" "Don't worry, I'm not making a mess." Victoria has figured out that if Jake comes home with a new tool, he must have had a bad day at work. One Thanksgiving morning Victoria was in the middle of getting the turkey into the oven when Jake decided to pull down the old kitchen cabinets and install new ones. The very cabinets that had been sitting in the garage for five months, he decided to install on Thanksgiving morning. It took Victoria a few more years of remodeling projects to figure out that Jake gets anxious about entertaining, and his way of coping is to take a hammer to something. Now she tricks him by warning him weeks in advance so that he can get started.

The remodeling disorder is a prevalent symptom of male middlescence. Gail's husband has it, too. Around dinnertime one evening, he decided to remodel the bathroom. His intention was to put in a Jacuzzi tub and double shower. "It's your birthday present," he told her. While she did appreciate his generous gesture, she didn't appreciate that the floor, toilet, tub, and walls were out of commission for more than two months. When she finally threatened to hire a contractor, he finished the job in a week.

What it comes down to is that we all have our moods.

What it comes down to is that we all have our moods. Men are as nervous around our crying jags as we are around their fits of carpentry. After thirty-one years of marriage, Victoria has found the best way to manage Jake's moods. "I stay out of the way while he is starting the project, and when I want to make a suggestion I say it slowly and calmly, usually over dinner." I think Jake has figured out how to deal with Victoria, too. The other day I walked past their house and saw him on a ladder. "What are you doing?" I asked. "Getting ready to paint the trim," he answered. "What color?" I asked. "Oh, I don't pick out colors," he said. "You'll have to ask Victoria about that."

To Do or Not to Do

1. Repeat this over and over: Men and women are different. Women cry, men remodel.

2. Remember girls, men have middlescence moods, too. It's best not to point them out, however, especially in the middle of a remodeling job.

3. Encourage and acknowledge your sweetheart's handyman inclinations. You can rest, and he can remodel the house.

4. Make sure that the "Honey Do" list is long and complicated. Think of it as creative multitasking—you can get things done around the house and keep your husband busy at the same time.

5. Stock the house with plenty of dark chocolate and bubble bath.

If you live with a man going through middlescence, you're going to need it.

$$\overline{\qquad\qquad}$$

"The roosters may crow, but the hens deliver the goods."

—Ann Richards

A Woman's Word

Women are magnificent! Women are spunky, sensitive, sympathetic, and sassy. We are marvelous at any age, but during the second half of life we are fantastic. As girls we are energetic and imaginative and ready to take on the world. As young women we are bright and inventive and ready to change the world. By thirty-nine we are reaching for our potential. There is so much more to give, to receive, and to experience. We are honing our intentions, sharpening our interests, and discovering the fuel of our spirit. We are stretching beyond what others told us we should be. We are finding our voice and becoming more than what we thought we were—more radiant, more ingenious, more discerning. It is in the second half of life that we really start to shine.

Forty-, fifty-, and sixty-year-old women everywhere are renewing their dreams, appreciating their bodies, and following their creative impulses. These years are for polishing our talents, refining our intuition, and expressing our vision. We are out of the "something's wrong with me" box. We are moving away from "I'm not good enough" and the fits of self-loathing. We have abandoned the habit of comparing ourselves to the other women around us, in magazines, and on television. During these years, we begin to recognize that there is no need to compete with each other. We are recognizing that everything about being female is perfectly right. We trust our hearts, our minds, and our bodies. We are starting to understand what it means to really love ourselves. We enter these years holding our heads up high. We are desirable, enchanting, interesting, interested, realistic, optimistic, and resilient. We do not need to be told what to do; we decide for ourselves. We refuse to be silenced by age, society, or expectations. We refuse to grow stodgy, turn dowdy, or lower our aspirations.

> Women accomplish great things. We nurture our children, adore our men, and lift each other up.

Women accomplish great things. We nurture our children, adore our men, and lift each other up. We honor our fathers, our husbands, and our mothers for literally giving us life. We empower our children to take the best of us, improve on it, and become all that they can be. We make the ordinary lovely. We add zing. We are artistic and passionate. We care. We make things happen. We work hard and comfort one another. When we are bored, we admit it, consider it, reflect on what is needed, and change directions. We are creative. We cook, lift weights, give speeches, fight injustice, plant gardens, dance, ride motorcycles, paint walls, sing, write music, paint pictures, do the laundry, take on causes, and run institutions.

At midlife we make peace. We accept our bodies and soothe hurt feelings. We let go of resentment. We treasure talent and nurture our own talents as often as we can. We live with flair. We believe in goodness, stand for decency, restore the broken, forgive ourselves, and jump for joy. We reflect the heart of love, the essence of creativity, and the passion of a spirit on fire.

To Do or Not to Do

1. Innovate. Do not imitate. Be a passionate midlifer.
2. Pay your dues by forgiving yourself for all past boo-boos and errors in judgment. Beating yourself up drains your spark.
3. No squelching allowed. Develop all your talents. Bring out the parts of yourself that you once pushed aside.
4. Achieve your own dreams. That's the mark of a true original.
5. Print bumper stickers and spread the word: "Women are magnificent."

"You are enough. You are blessed. Hold nothing in."

—Patricia Lynn Reilly

Midlife Darlings

Are you into painting? Are you painting walls, front doors, and porch steps? Are you into vivid colors? Are you planting perennials, cooking with herbs, and drying lavender? Are you laughing in between hot flashes and memory lapses? Are you taking up yoga? Designing mosaics? Thinking about setting your inner poet free? Are you simplifying? Are you nonchalant about getting ahead? Are you lounging around? Are you noticing birds? Are you answering yes? Have you thought about writing? Then you positively have creative tendencies. Even though you may never have claimed your artistry or creative character, be assured that you can. Be assured that you have right brain proclivities. It is highly likely that you are a free spirit with an expressive temperament.

Irma admits to stifling her eloquent side. She squelches her passion and gives in to duty. She wants to write a novel, but so far she hasn't gotten around to writing even one tiny sentence. Instead, she attends school board meetings, collects for the library fund, and volunteers for the church building committee. She lets responsibilities encroach on her creative time. Irma is conscientious about giving back to her community, but that isn't satisfying her creative urges. She is reluctant to resign from what she does so well in order to dive into something that she's never done. Irma is one of those all or nothing women. She expects herself to be perfect or she won't tackle it. Fortunately, she's only forty-seven and she can sense that an attitude shift is coming.

> To be an artist, a writer, a poet, a decorator, or to be a gourmet of any kind, you have to be willing to be a beginner.

Anything worth doing well is worth beginning. Whenever we begin any new art form the learning curve is steep, and we make mistakes and get frustrated. To be an artist, a writer, a poet, a decorator, or to be a gourmet of any kind, you have to be willing to be a beginner. You have to make friends with mistakes. As young women we often took our artistic mistakes seriously; we thought they were labels, and we often felt ashamed for making them. We compared ourselves to others, and sometimes we were so discouraged that we stopped doing art. Some of us didn't even know that we had artistic leanings, and we doubted our talent. As grown-up women we know that releasing our inner artist is not a task, but a pleasurable process. If we make a mistake in the art of living or in expressing our artistic side, we will make adjustments and begin again. Yes, we are shocked by cellulite and getting older, but we've moved past complaining about it. Midlife darlings don't have time for grumbling. We have walls to paint and rooms to decorate. We have projects. We have to inspire young women. We cannot compare or compete with younger women. Instead, we must support young women totally. Our hearts must go out to them. We must take them in our arms and tell them how beautiful and talented they are. We must tell them that we appreciate their youthful bodies and their drive. We must let them know that our only regret is that we were not able to appreciate our own youthful bodies while we had them. We've learned that lesson, too, and are appreciating the bodies we have now.

We nurture, pamper, listen to, and coddle our darling spirit. Whatever intrigues us, we follow that. We will resign from duties and schedule creative time. We will guard our creativity carefully. That's how it is done. If we want to paint, we have to make an appointment to paint. We will make messes and embrace those messes as part of the learning process. If we want to be writers, we must first write mediocre sentences and later smooth them into funny, touching, delightful ones.

Nobody is judging us, because we don't let them. There are no gatekeepers. No one is standing over our shoulder saying, "You can't do that." We may not know what we are doing, but that is exactly why we do it. We are passionately creative, utterly artistic, and aesthetically shaped. We are over fifty, free, and oh so darling.

To Do or Not to Do

1. Recite this: "Anything worth doing is worth beginning."
2. Be a beginner. Recite this motto: "I may not know what I'm doing, but that is exactly why I do it."
3. Admire young women. Encourage them to appreciate their beautiful bodies and talents. Be a living example of a woman who appreciates her own.
4. Resign from some of your duties and schedule creative time. Do it as if your genius depends on it. It does.
5. Make your own plans. Don't let others make them for you.

Show Your Colors

Whether you're painting one wall or wearing black, just a touch of color can say and do so much.

> **RAVISHING RED** is passionate, the color of romance. Ms. Red has love in her heart and excitement in her veins. She's vivacious and lively. She's strong and feisty with a stubborn streak. She gets attention (that's why stop signs and fire engines are fiery red). A splash of red is quite sensuous. Just think of red lips, red nails, and red-light districts, and you'll know what I mean.

> **SERENE GREEN** is soothing, the color of freshness. Ms. Green has harmony in her heart and hope in her veins. She is a natural, a beginner with a jealous streak. Being with her is soothing, and she is trustworthy. That's why green traffic lights mean go ahead, it's safe. A splash of green is quite pleasant and motivating. After all, green is the color of money. Watch out though— too much and you might look greedy.

> **SASSY ORANGE** is enthusiastic, the color of encouragement. Ms. Orange has joy in her heart and determination in her veins. She is spunky, creative, and independent. Whatever she wants, she goes for it. If you're prone to hot flashes, do not wear too much orange, because Ms. Orange may get your blood rushing and you'll feel even hotter. A tinge of orange, however, encourages healthy eating and allows you to think more clearly.

> **CHEERY YELLOW** is happy, the color of joy. Ms. Yellow has merriment in her heart and bliss in her veins. She is spontaneous with a playful side. She can get carried away, and she draws attention. Just think of yellow marking pens

highlighting the paper. If you want to get noticed, a little bit goes a long way. She is frisky. If you have grandchildren, watch out, because too much yellow can make young ones jittery.

> **HEALING BLUE** is compassionate, the color of wisdom. Ms. Blue has peace in her heart and confidence in her veins. She is wise, truthful, loyal, and trustworthy. She is calm and tranquil, although she can be slightly pious. She is sincere but may get carried away with cleanliness. Blue is attractive to men, associated with consciousness and intellect. Too much blue, and you might feel slightly stodgy or bored.

> **PASSIONATE PURPLE** is extravagant, the color of mystery. Ms. Purple has creativity in her heart and magic in her veins. She is dignified, independent, and noble. Ms. Purple is full of energy, a romantic with nostalgic leanings. A touch of purple gives the impression of wealth and royalty. And just a hint also brings out the feminine side. If she gets dark, however, she tends to be gloomy and sad. And remember, a little goes a long way.

> **NOT-SO-SIMPLE WHITE** is innocent, the color of purity. Ms. White has light in her heart and goodness in her veins. She is safe and sweet. She gives the impression of virginity, but that is not the complete picture. She's aloof with a seductive side. She's hard to know yet welcoming to other colors. She is often associated with angels, but she has a mischievous side.

> **SOPHISTICATED BLACK** is refined, the color of elegance. Ms. Black has mystery in her heart and power in her veins. She is alluring, secretive, and overflowing with good taste. She oozes prestige. When combined with bright colors, she makes a powerful statement. She likes formality. A symbol of grief, Ms. Black walks a fine line between heartache and determination.

Section Two . . .

Atrocities, Growing Up,
and Other Victories

Growing up is incredibly shocking. We thought we were finished, but we find out that we are works in progress. When we discover that we are older than we think we are, we have a few terrifying moments. It is scary! The fact that our doctor, our lawyer, and our neighbors are the age of our children is enough to send us right over our everlasting, youthful edge. But hang on, baby! We have achieved some of our dreams but not all of them. We have artistic intentions and are transported by them. Our future is not predestined. Moment by delicate moment we happily design it.

Age Does Not Define a Woman

When it comes to expressing ourselves creatively some of us are late bloomers, but that does not stop us because we know that age does not define who we are or who we can become. It is our spunky attitude that defines who we are. Each of us is on our very own path and our very own timetable. It does not matter how old we are, it only matters how alive we are. It does not matter who we thought we were last decade, it only matters who we are today. What we are drawn to is our compass. That is the direction to travel.

Cecile studied dance in college but gave it up when she got married. She daydreams about dancing again, and when she sees a movie or a performance with dancing in it, she cries. That is her clue to take it up again. Whatever we have been drawn to in the past and whatever we are drawn to in the present is our signal that there is something waiting for us.

Simone has been a wannabe makeup artist since she began painting the faces of her playmates at age four. When she saw the six-week evening class offered in Makeup Artistry on a local campus, she was so excited that she couldn't breathe. She jumped up and down. She knew she was onto something and she threw caution to the wind, filled out the registration form, and was ready. She was the oldest student by about twenty years, but it didn't discourage her from playing. She was amused and noticed that the other students were quite impressed by her gumption. She knew better than to compare herself to them. She was on her own path and on her own timetable. Instead of focusing on age differences or taking herself seriously, she learned the tips, tricks, and techniques that enhance facial features. She's having a ball doing makeovers on her girlfriends and they are tickled pink to be playing along. Simone is gaining understanding of facial anatomy and color theory and has found the best brushes for the job. She may apply for a part-time job at the makeup counter, but she won't do it unless it's fun. She is too wise not to have fun while playing. Simone is thinking about volunteering to do the stage makeup for the community theater.

It does not matter what age we are when we start expressing our artistic side. Opportunity knocks when the time is right. The teacher appears, the class is there, and we can sign up. Age has nothing to do with it. We can be absorbed and play at any stage. There are no age limits for rediscovering dance or for putting on makeup. Whatever age we are, we are beautiful as long as we are alive, lively, and playing with makeup.

To Do or Not to Do

1. Repeat after me: "Age does not define a woman. Age does not define a woman."

2. Give yourself permission to play with makeup. Buy a makeup brush.
3. Have a makeover party with your girlfriends. Makeovers are fun at any age.
4. Pay close attention to what artistic expression you are drawn to. Chances are there is something there for you to explore.
5. Get tickled pink and play along. Follow your own path.

"Deep down, I'm pretty superficial."

—Ava Gardner

Medical Jargon and Yadda, Yadda, Yadda

You know that you have arrived at middlescence when you start talking about bodily fluids and bodily functions with your girlfriends over lunch.

"I hate the word menopause," Meg announces. "I hate the sound, the looks, and the connotation. It gives me the willies, and I refuse to wrap myself in it." Kristen agrees and avoids using the word, too. "Can you imagine Elaine from *Seinfeld* using *that* word?" Meg asks. "Nope," Kristen answers, "Elaine would never use that word." And they really like Elaine. So instead, Meg and Kristen have established a protocol to cover the subject: "If we need to talk about 'it,' we say 'the M thing!' "

Their friend Ann is a holistic nurse practitioner. She thinks Meg and Kristen are slightly deranged, but she loves them anyway. "They're perimenopause," she says and pushes beyond their reluctance. "The word *meis* comes from the Greek, meaning moon, and from the French word *pause*, meaning pause," she instructs. "That's negative!" Kristen screams. "I refuse to put my life on pause."

Mention a twinge, a twitch, a throb, a cramp, a hot flash, or a flutter and Ann is looking at your tongue and taking your pulse. She has horror stories about blood clots and lumps that will turn a perfectly wonderful shopping trip into a medical exam. She can diagnose hormone imbalances, heavy bleeding, painful breasts, and fibroids over lunch. Objections do not deter her, she happily prescribes herbal remedies for all womanly conditions—PMS or perimenopausal. Supplements for acne, teas for insomnia, stress reduction techniques for fatigue and mood swings. Symptoms and conditions are her passion. She is on a mission to heal. "It's good to be informed, primed, and balanced," she teaches. "Growth hormones are the latest." "Enough already," Kristen says. "Down with medical jargon, up with nonsense." Meg and Kristen put their hands over their ears and recite in unison, "Yadda, yadda, yadda."

That's one of the perks of having M-stage girlfriends. You can all be as outrageous, as adamant, as independent, or as silly as you like. You can resort to all kinds of stunts, make up your own rules, be neurotic if it suits your fancy, diagnose your friends, and laugh about it. "We're not as influenced by what others think as we once were," Meg says. "No, we're just neurotic," Kristen adds. "Neurotic and cute like Elaine." They'd rather talk about what they're doing and where they're going than judge each other. They'd rather ponder great thoughts, watch *Seinfeld* reruns, and cry at movies than compete. They'd rather join causes and spread kindness. They've given up on perfection and embraced the poetic. They prefer shopping, lunching, and humoring each other.

When you complain about your aches and pains and find out that all your girlfriends are having similar twinges, it is as if you've become a member of a society of understanding sisters. You have more in common than you ever wanted to.

What a great philosophy! A holistic approach that combines denial with medical conditions, menopause, and hormones. When you complain about your aches and pains and find out that all your girlfriends are having similar twinges, it is as if you've become a member of a society of understanding sisters. You have more in common than you ever wanted to. It's a relief to be able to confide in each other. Then you can all take a trip to the ladies room before and after lunch and share information about bladder exercises.

Take some herbal tea, infuse it with the poetic, add a dose of laughter and you've got a prescription worth trying. Girlfriends, bodily functions, remedies, and a surplus of opinions. Accept what fits for you, ignore the rest, order lunch, throw in a splash of medical jargon, and yadda, yadda, yadda.

To Do or Not to Do

1. Rename medical terms to suit your fancy.
2. If you don't feel like revealing your entire condition say, "It's the 'M' thing and yadda, yadda, yadda."
3. Put a sitcom spin on your day. Describe what you're going through as Elaine might.
4. If someone diagnoses you as neurotic, consider it a compliment. After all, it's those quirks that make you so adorable.
5. Take care of yourself with holistic remedies and a dose of denial.

"The statistics on sanity are that one out of every four
Americans are suffering from some form of mental illness.
Think of your three best friends. If they're OK, then it's you."

—RITA MAE BROWN

Invisible Lady

Here I am at the age of maturity and I don't get it. No one sees me anymore. It's not that I need or want to be the center of attention, but an occasional wink thrown my way might be nice. These days my daughter gets all of the glances.

In my thirties, when Manda was a toddler, I was delighted and entertained by the attention she received. "Look at those curls," a shopper might say. "Oh, what big, blue eyes," they'd say admiringly. Manda was willing to play peek-a-boo with any friendly face. Riding in the stroller, she'd wiggle, wave, and grin. It was her baby way of flirting and it came naturally. It was intrinsic to being a girl. Grandfathers would wink and grandmothers would coo. Manda liked the game. I'd smile, nod, and we'd continue on our way. New faces, happy attention—being playful could turn ordinary errands into a fun connection. "Your baby is so cute" was an affirmation that she was a "chip off the old mom block."

As Manda grew older I reveled in all her successes. "She's a little go-getter," the third grade soccer coach told me. "She's got spunk," the fifth grade teacher announced. "You and your daughter have a great relationship," the junior high counselor noted. There was plenty of jovial feedback to go around. Whenever I'd pick Manda up from school, her classmates waved and said, "Hi Judy." In high school, when friends dropped over to visit her, they'd stop in the kitchen first to say hello to me. It was fun to be included.

At sixteen, Manda was a knockout. And I'm not just saying that because I'm her mother! Her grandfather and uncles confirmed my observation. "She's going to break a few hearts," they teased. I took pride in their warnings. Signs of the inevitable were everywhere. By the time I was fifty-one it was becoming increasingly obvious. Whatever sexual allure I once had, I was in a new phase and passing the baton to my daughter.

For example, Manda and I went to dinner and the maitre d', closer to my age than hers, looked right passed me and asked her, "How many in your party?" "Two," she answered. "How nice that you're dining with your mother," he smiled half-heartedly, pulling out my chair while conversing with her about the good weather. "He's old enough to be her father," I thought, "but at least he's got good taste." The twenty-something waiter couldn't contain himself, either, and practically stood on his head to charm her. "Are you ready to order?" he asked her first. "Mom, you go ahead," she said. "Salmon," I said. I couldn't blame him for turning his wiles toward her. He was a gorgeous, healthy young man, and she was a lovely young girl. I've had my moments. This one belonged to them.

My days of turning heads and breaking hearts are ending. Over the hill, sexually ineligible, screened out, no longer a catch. I'm getting the message. My little girl has become a lovely young woman, a knock-out, a beauty, a prize. It's her turn to get the whistles. She is the belle of the ball. I brag about her, laugh about it, complain about it, understand the reason behind it, and yet there's a melancholy sting. I'm thrilled for her, and I wish there were still a few whistles for me.

"We're just older and that's not our fault."

"Ahh well," my friend Nora, who has a gorgeous sixteen-year-old daughter of her own, sympathizes. "We'll just have to turn our heads in another direction and focus there." "Yeah," I agree, "that's what we'll do, it can't be too hard." "There are perks to that, too," she encourages. "At least we know that the reason we aren't attracting the men is because we're old—it isn't because we aren't still sexy or intriguing or knockouts." "That's right," I say. "We're just older and that's not our fault."

To Do or Not to Do

1. Repeat in unison: "We are middle aged and that is not our fault."
2. Accept the truth! You are feeling left out, over the hill, invisible, and a little sad about it.
3. Go out to dinner with someone your own age. Reminisce about the days when you could turn heads, too.
4. Go to the library and read poetry by Judith Viorst. One of her books will make a great gift for a friend who is suffering from the invisible curse.
5. Yes, you are becoming invisible, but think about the advantages of that!

"I'm trying very hard to understand this generation.
They have adjusted the timetable for childbearing so
that menopause and teaching a sixteen-year-old how
to drive a car will occur in the same week."

—ERMA BOMBECK

The Advantages of Being Invisible

Life begins at forty. We have heard it said a thousand times. When we are thirty-nine and freaking out about being over the hill, we are skeptical about that little phrase. Life begins at forty? Impossible. It must be an advertising slogan for wrinkle cream, antacids, or arthritis medication. At thirty-nine we are so shaky about hitting the big 4-0 that some of us start lying about our age. To avoid being forty some of us subject our bodies to all kinds of unpleasant procedures, from Botox to liposuction, to extreme makeovers. Life begins at forty? How could it be? we wonder. Then we hit forty-nine, and by that age we have started to grasp that the advantages of being over forty go hand in hand with being invisible. That is why so many women in their fifties and sixties are saying, "These are the very best years of my life."

The advantages of being over forty go hand in hand with being invisible.

Being invisible is not a condition Isabelle accepted readily. It took a couple of years for her to comprehend that she could use invisibility on her own behalf. As a young girl Isabelle had often pretended to be invisible. She liked being a girl detective and spying on her brothers. "If I were invisible I could have so much freedom. I could do anything, go anywhere, and no one would notice. I could wear pajamas to school or chew gum in class. The teacher wouldn't be able to call on me to recite if she couldn't see me. I could follow my brothers on their dates and learn all kinds of things about boys." As a young girl Isabelle was sure that being invisible would save her from the unnecessary inconveniences that go with being seen.

Isabelle forgot about her childhood wish until somewhere around age forty-seven, when she noticed that she was indeed turning invisible. "I noticed it first at the deli. When the clerk waited on me, she was polite but she looked right past me to the younger woman standing beside me. It was a subtle message that happened over and over." Clerks, waiters, and all kind of strangers responded to her requests, but it was as if she wasn't there. "If I wanted to make small talk, I would have to initiate it." That same year Isabelle painted the front porch red. "I think I was trying to make a statement and be noticed."

As astonishing as a red porch might be, arriving at a certain age and turning invisible is even more startling. Fortunately, with advance preparation for the inevitable and with experience under our middle-aged belts, we eventually come to appreciate the following benefits:

1. You can do anything you want and no one seems to notice or care. If they do notice what you are doing, they are usually pleasantly surprised that a woman of your age is so intriguing.
2. You can go to the store without makeup because you know that no one is looking closely at your face.
3. You can slip into the movie alone and be assured that no one is talking about you.
4. You know that when people like you, it is for who you are, not how you look.
5. You do not threaten women, so it is easier to make new friends.
6. You can relax more because you do not have to perform.
7. You can watch other people very closely without them noticing that you are. You can go to a cocktail party and no one expects you to make small talk.
8. You can have a cranky day without pretending to be cheerful.
9. You can put your creative energy into pleasing yourself instead of pleasing others.
10. When you choose to be noticed, you can say something brilliant and shock the pants right off the most dignified folks. When you speak up, they will look at you with respect. In fact, they will usually stop in their tracks and give you the appreciation that you deserve. They will be embarrassed that they

ignored such a lovely, fascinating creature as you. They will go out of their way to make it up to you. Isabella says, "Play it up to the hilt."

To Do or Not to Do

1. Practice being invisible. Slip into a movie and notice that no one is watching you.
2. Watch closely and you will see that some people really do see you. They see the real you. This is good information for you to have because these evolved souls are worth knowing.
3. Acknowledge invisible men and women. Say something like, "You can't hide, I see who you are."
4. Experiment. Go without makeup for one day. See if it makes any difference in how you are treated by others.
5. Pour your energy into what you pleases you, not in pleasing others.

"She too is round, losing her waist to children and the responsibilities of middle age. But she enters the dance with abandon, her hips joyously in sync with the wild cadences that fill the room."

—BARBARA HERRICK

Body Part Management

"I have a whole new relationship to my body," says forty-five-year-old Greta. Since Greta turned forty-five, she goes to great lengths to avoid getting sick. She never fakes it like she used to. When Greta was a kid, she was an expert at imitating stomachaches. "Mom, I'm going to throw up," she would whimper on her sprint to the bathroom. There, leaning over the toilet she could feign such a perfect, wrenching sound that her mother would insist that she stay home from school. As a young adult, Greta was good at conning herself into the flu. Any woozy twinge was all the proof she would need to lounge in bed for a few days. But since she turned forty-five, she has stopped pretending. The tiniest twitch makes her nervous. It could be serious, and that she does not want.

Body part management is a huge issue and it gets trickier as we get older. Every twinge makes us wonder if we are getting sick, and every muscle ache reminds us that our bodies are aging. We walk a fine line between going to the doctor and pushing through. "I've got more body parts than I knew I had," Greta comments. She's recently discovered skin tags. In case you don't know what skin tags are, they are tiny, benign skin protrusions that occur most often at midlife. They are annoying and they pop out in unexpected places like the neck and torso. Greta is not big on yearly checkups, but she wants those pesky skin tags on her eyelids frozen off. Her reason for not visiting the doctor: "I object to wearing a tiny blue paper gown." If we're going to get over the angst of going to the doctor, then some creative woman like Donna Karan or Eileen Fisher should design a flattering gown for us to wear while we're waiting for our x-rays.

Our midlife quest includes a new relationship with our bodies. From bones to breasts, from skin to joints, it seems like there are more parts to manage. Our reflexes slow, we get a questionable test result from a mammogram, our skin is thinner, and we may find a sun-caused age spot on our hands or face. We are warned about our bones. Many of us have disconnected from our bodies and don't recognize warning signs when we feel them. Some of us have even hate our shape; comparing ourselves to younger women, we starve ourselves into submission. We know there's a relationship between stress and illness, but we don't always handle our stress very well.

Body parts can be our guide. What is your body telling you? "If I want to be healthy and live a long life, I have to be friends with all my parts." Greta is trusting her instincts, listening to her body's wisdom, and taking care of it. If she is stressed, she knows that if she doesn't deal with it, the stress will show up in her body. Life expectancy is creeping upward and the disability rate is falling. We do not need to suffer from sickness, hysteria, or helpless dread. "I rest when I need to and I don't fake symptoms to do it." Greta has decided, "There's a connection between my thoughts and my body and I'm keeping them positive."

"There's a connection between my thoughts and my body and I'm keeping them positive."

To Do or Not to Do

1. Make friends with all your body parts.
2. Listen for the body's messages. If your body is aching, that is a message.
3. Rest when you need or want to. You don't need to fake illness or get sick to take it easy.
4. Take as good care of your body as you do your pets, your lover, and your children.
5. Go for 100. Society tells us that we get sicker as we age; don't believe it.

"Many people can listen to their cat more intelligently than they can listen to their own despised body."

—MARION WOODMAN

Reflections on a Face-Lift

My best friend Jean and I have on several occasions discussed our sagging neckline. We have stood side by side at the mirror and pulled the skin back just above our jawline. We agree we could use a little tuck. Neither one of us wants one of those all-over face lifts that make you look like you've been stretched so tight that you can't close your eyes. We don't want the results to be obvious, and since we can't be guaranteed that we will like the results, neither one of us has gone under the knife. We have accepted that there must be reasons that the Almighty invented aging. My friend Jean says it best:

"I have a feeling that after putting myself through the ordeal (it's got to be an ordeal, from searching out a surgeon that you hope won't butcher you, to sitting in the office and having your face or body critiqued up close and personal, to the inevitable presurgical anxiety, followed by the post-op pain), I would probably end up disappointed.

"Even if I thought, 'Gee, I look refreshed and perky,' the fantasy of having a procedure to give me a more youthful appearance might somehow include a mistaken sense that I will physically and mentally turn back the clock. I might fool myself into believing that I have a second chance at youth. I can see myself falling into the fantasy that my whole life is before me, which of course it is, but not in the way that it was when I was younger. By centering my focus on trying to regain at least the appearance of youth, I may be losing out on a very important and special time in my life. If I refuse to accept that being fifty or sixty is just as valuable and

>>>

interesting and full of meaning as being a thirty-year-old, maybe I'll miss the blessings of this stage. If I give my attention to uplifting my jowls over my inner self, I might not fully engage in where I am now. I might never reap what this special time has to teach me. Sure, there is another side to that coin, which pulls me in the other way. That is why I have always been a creature of indecision."

—Jean Theisen, my very best friend

Desires at Fifteen and Fifty

Sex and desire are complicated for all of us—especially at fifteen and fifty. Do widows do it? What about midlifers? Do they think about it? Do it? At midlife, we're often surprised that our desires are stronger than ever. That's why Norah is reading *Everything Your Kid Wants to Know About Sex and You're Afraid They'll Ask*. She's the proud mom of a teenage girl, and she's getting more comfortable with the subject, beginning to see desire—her own and her daughter's—as natural.

Middle age is swimming with conundrums. Just when you think the problem is *her* hormones, you find out that *your* hormones are raging too. If you're a menopausal woman with a teenager, you're going to learn plenty about hormones and sexuality. When you're in your forties or fifties and living with a teenage daughter, the chances are certain that you'll come face to face with desires—both yours and hers. Welcome to the wild mouse ride.

If you're a menopausal woman with a teenager, you're going to learn plenty about hormones and sexuality.

Norah walked into the den and found her fifteen-year-old daughter Allie on top of her boyfriend, a seventeen-year-old boy named Parker. Everyone was startled. Allie jumped up and pulled down her blouse. Parker jumped up and pulled up his jeans. Norah walked out of the room. She was mad and scared, but she wasn't exactly sure what to do about it. At fifty, she was facing the same doubts and desires that she once had when she was her daughter's age. Sometimes she felt like a teenager herself. She wanted to give good guidance to her daughter, but she didn't know how. She wasn't sure where to begin. She decided to begin with herself.

After her husband Phil died of an unexpected cerebral hemorrhage, Norah poured all her passion into parenting. She was diligent about that; after all, she was both mom and dad. Perhaps that's her justification for snooping around and reading her daughter's e-mails. And even though it caused her anguish when she did it, she hadn't been able to stop. All those e-mails about sucking and licking were driving Norah wild. That was her clue. It was time to consider handling the issues directly instead of hoping they would go away. What is acceptable behavior for a fifteen-year-old? What is acceptable for a fifty-year-old widow?

Being the single parent of a fifteen-year-old-girl in the throes of blossoming desire has required more soul-searching from Norah than she ever imagined. At fifty years old, Norah is still grappling with left-over guilt from a proper Catholic upbringing. Norah thought that was behind her, but seeing her daughter's budding sexuality stirs her own confusion. "With a teenager at home, I am finding out how low I can really sink. She screams at me, 'Just leave me alone, you can't stop me!' and there I am, screaming right back, 'As long as you're living under my roof, you're not doing that!'" Norah is finding out how much she has to learn about talking with her daughter about sensitive subjects, and in the process, she's learning about herself.

Trying to help a daughter figure out something that you haven't figured out for yourself is heart-wrenching. Norah loves her daughter and so she's courageously looking deeply at her own guilt, rage, and inhibitions. "My goal is to be sexually liberated by sixty," she says. Norah is hanging around older women as a way to do her own sex research. She wants to know from older women about their desire, how they manage it, and how they wished they would have managed it. She wants to talk about fifteen- and fifty- and seventy-year-old urges. She's tired of pretending the hunger doesn't exist. "I want to liberate myself from what we never really talk about and the secrets we keep from each other." Norah wants to find out, What do women of a certain age do with desire? How do you talk intelligently and gently about sex with your daughter? What do you do with your own sadness and desire when there's no partner? How do you give good guidance?

It's in facing our own sexuality that we find the way to understand and really be there for our daughters. It is by understanding ourselves that we can see our way clear to give good guidance. By the time she's sixty, Norah wants to be free from shame and guilt. She wants to be gentle with desire and be there for her daughter. Norah wants to celebrate all those fledgling steps—her daughter's and her own. She wants to celebrate aliveness.

To Do or Not to Do

1. See the documentary *Still Doing It!*
2. Talk to your liberated friends. If you don't have any liberated folks around, get some.
3. Diagnose yourself. If you are snooping, prying, controlling, losing sleep, poking fun, and screaming, you've got raging hormones and you need good counsel.

4. Be gentle with yourself so that you can be gentle with your daughter. She needs understanding, kindness, acceptance, and guidance. If you don't know the answers, find out.

5. Celebrate aliveness! Plan a mother-daughter outing. Do something exciting and new together.

"I once had a rose named after me and I was very flattered.
But I was not pleased to read the description in the catalogue:
'not good in a bed, but fine up against a wall.'"

—ELEANOR ROOSEVELT

Zesty Cars

For ten years, I've been imagining myself driving around in a convertible. I picture cruising Lake Washington Boulevard with the top down. Sun shining, cool air blowing my hair, there I am listening to Elton John and tapping my fingers on the steering wheel. "A convertible isn't practical in Seattle," I remind myself. "That's why you bought a Honda Accord." An Accord is respectable and dependable, and mine has a sunroof. I like it, but it's not the same as a ragtop. I considered trading it in last year for a VW convertible, but I vacillated. Besides, should a woman my age be driving a Beetle, like she did thirty years ago?

My first car, a bright yellow Volkswagen convertible bug with a black ragtop, was a knockout, a real cutie. I adored her. Bumper to bumper, Ms. Sunshine was loaded with personality. A charmer from every angle—top up or top down. At twenty-five years old, I felt grown up behind the wheel. I managed my finances and made payments on time. I took responsibility for her check-ups and polished her chassis. We roamed California freeways and beaches together; she was my buddy. Even driving to my social work job at the Department of Public Assistance was thrilling. Yes, I was a grown woman with a real job, a real life, and real problems, but riding with top down was enough to convince me that with the right car, grownups don't have to be stodgy or stuffy.

Ms. Sunshine and I survived the sudden death of my first husband and a grief-filled rebound marriage to my second. When she was ten years old, however, she was so feeble that I had to trade her in. I was sad to let her go.

My second car was elegant, a white convertible bug with a white ragtop. She was one of a kind, a limited edition with special rims and a white interior. She was classy, a unique beauty, dignified but not snooty. That car was pretty as a princess and I felt like royalty, which was paradoxical since I was drowning in bills from the demise of my second marriage. The Princess lifted me up and I didn't feel so downtrodden. After eight years, she grew frail and I couldn't afford to keep her going. Everything needed replacing. I put so much money into her that when the steering went, I had to make a decision: Keep getting her fixed or trade her in for something practical.

I was a mother raising a daughter. The Civic hatchback was in my price range, with a solid image, dependable, but not much fun; a trouper, but ho-hum. Next I had a Toyota that I eventually passed down to Amanda. Then I bought the black Accord. It's a perfectly nice car. Respectable. Dependable. Predictable.

But here's my situation: I have PMZ (postmenopausal zest).

I have PMZ.

    post . . .

        menopausal . . .

            zest . . .

Menopause is designated by the date of our final period. PMZ is that "go for the gusto" desire that swells up afterward. We spend the first half of adulthood juggling so many responsibilities, driving reasonable cars, and dressing for success, that once we pass through menopause we want to spice ourselves up again. My friend Gabriel is debating between a Jaguar and a Prius. She's deciding between a racy persona and an environmentally conscious one. We women have numerous sides to our personalities, and choosing a car to match all our alter egos is huge. We might long to present a conservative, proper image in a Mercedes sedan while at the same time our flamboyant and outdoorsy side yearns for a Jeep.

I have a sassy side and I think a convertible bug expresses it best. But then my sensible side kicks in—there's absolutely nothing wrong with my Honda. It has low mileage, looks good, runs perfectly, and, besides, it's a "grownup" car. If I indulge my whims and get a Beetle, will I look silly, like the bald guys who drive red sports cars? For the most part, I no longer get wrapped up in restrictive thinking, but if I'm really honest there are still those corners of my psyche that want to be respected and look dignified. I want to accept my age with grace and not get caught up in holding on to the past. And I'm doing that by sticking with the Honda, right? I just don't know. That's my dilemma. I've got PMZ and a youthful outlook. I'm a grownup. I'm dignified. But I'm also spunky and ready to throw caution to the wind. Perhaps I'm ready for a car that reflects those qualities—a modern-day version of Ms. Sunshine. If there is a moral of the story, it is this: I have not made up my mind yet about the car I want to drive next and I don't have to. Life is open-ended and I have don't have to decide right now. I can wait and mull it over. I can wait until the right car comes along. I have lived long enough to know that when the time is right, the car that fits my personality will probably appear.

To Do or Not to Do

1. Buy a car that reflects the real you. Buy a car that expresses either your snazzy persona or your environmentally conscious side. If you can't decide between the two, buy them both.
2. Describe your alter egos. The better you can identify all your personalities, the better prepared you will be to explain to the car salesman the type of car you're looking for.
3. Be zesty. If anyone questions your actions, tell them, "I can't help it, it's PMZ" (postmenopausal zest).
4. Honk and wave to all the zesty drivers.
5. Advise me. Should I trade in the Honda for a VW? Do you have another suggestion? E-mail me: judy@judyford.com.

"You are only young once, but you can stay immature indefinitely!"

—OGDEN NASH

Sex after Forty

Sex after forty is different from sex before forty. OK, so I'm not an expert on the subject, but even so, I'm fairly certain that the statement is accurate. The myth that we lose our interest as we grow older is based on the recognition that younger people are ready and willing at a moment's notice. They'll take all opportunities that come along, whether they're standing in line for a hamburger or sitting in the front seat of the car they just borrowed from their parents to go to the mall. I have never seen a forty-year-old do that! But that doesn't mean we have lost interest.

Sure, we learned about the birds and the bees during our adolescence, but where do we go to learn about sex in our middlescence? An acquaintance of mine—a mother of two who returned to college in her fifties and took a human sexuality course at a local university. She said it is the most popular class for freshmen. She barely made it in. She said the students sometimes asked questions about what was natural and unnatural. I think that doing something you like to do is natural. Doing something you *don't* like to do is *unnatural.* And if you have to experiment once or twice to discover what you like and what you don't like, that would appear to me as *extremely* natural. If in middlescence we want to experiment like we did when we were younger, why not?

When the kids are grown and out of the house, we can embrace our sensuality like we couldn't when we were parenting. If it's silky sheets and a porno flick that turns you on, you can partake without worrying about the kids down the hall. Single women can experiment, too. Women in their fifties are dating younger men, just like men have been doing for years.

By the time we are forty, we know more about our bodies, our partners, and our preferences. Wise women do not blame their men. We know that lovemaking does not have to be perfect every time, and we know that there will be times when it will be as good or better than it was when we were young. We know that good sex is not about doing it right or performing well. Good sex is more about connecting, having a good time, and playing. A grown-up woman is not going to have a hissy about her man coming too soon. She doesn't take it personally if he doesn't have an erection. We are more willing and less demanding. We have discovered that foreplay can last for hours. It can energize you more and more and then even more. And after an hour or two of foreplay, you can feel so contented that there's hardly a need for afterplay—or anything else. We know that we won't necessarily feel like making love at the same time, and we are more understanding about that, too. We are more caring, we give more slack, and we let the other person rest.

We are not so serious. We know that as soon as lovemaking becomes serious, it becomes work—and we have done enough work at the office. By the time we're fifty, sex is no longer about procreation, but rejuvenation. If we don't want to, we're able to say so, and when we're in the mood, we're able to communicate that, too. We are comfortable in our own skin and more connected with our partner because we're more connected to ourselves.

How do you surrender when your back hurts? What do you do when you hold your stomach in, but it's still sticking out? How do you look sexy when your sinuses are running? The only thing I've figured out for sure is this: Sex is not a serious subject.

We are becoming more playful each year, we laugh a lot more. Sex and laughter go together. Sweet sex just naturally brings up bubbling laughter in you. Suddenly you laugh at existence, even at yourself. And it isn't even that anything is really funny. You laugh because life seems so simple, so easy. Worries that you had just an hour ago are totally gone. How do you surrender when your back hurts? What do you do when you hold your stomach in, but it's still sticking out? How do you look sexy when your sinuses are running? The only thing I've figured out for sure is this: sex is not a serious subject. Important yes, serious no. A person who has a healthy interest in sex is not a serious person. A person like that may be lighthearted, loving, caring, tender, good natured, and playful, but not serious. Seriousness and good sex don't mix. So even if you cannot get in those super-duper twisted positions, you can still try and then laugh about it.

To Do or Not to Do

1. For those of you who are married, you might want to check out the book *Rekindling Desire: A Step-by-Step Program to Help Low-Sex and No-Sex Marriages* by Barry and Emily McCarthy. Talk about self-help!

2. For those of you who don't have a partner and are looking for a creative approach to find one, check out *A Round-Heeled Woman: My Late-Life Adventures in Sex and Romance* by Jane Juska. Talk about creative!

3. For those of you who are temporarily in your celibate phase, check out *Everyday Matters: A New York Diary* by Danny Gregory. Talk about inspiring!

4. Go to a comedy club. A good belly laugh loosens up the throat and the pelvis. Talk about exercise!

5. Learn something. Call the nearest university and sign up for the sex course. Talk about education!

"Sex is wonderful. Sex is delight.
Sex is about as close to God as we can usually get!"
—WILLIAM ASHOKA ROSS

Rebels with Pizzazz

Hooray! We've grown into ourselves. We are rebels with pizzazz. Roxie is. She hasn't had a hard life, but it hasn't been a bed of roses either. She is single after thirty-some years of marriage. She didn't think she could survive a divorce, but somehow she turned her sorrow into deep and creative living. She's an alchemist. She's hot-blooded, occasionally unruly, and feisty. Roxie takes on causes. She rocks the boat. Every Wednesday she dresses in black and joins other women in a silent vigil for peace. She makes peace signs in her garage and takes them to all the demonstrations. She won't be squelched or dominated. She prefers honoring life to destroying it. "It's better to do something," she says, "than fading away or hiding." If you ever hang out with Roxie or a woman like her, you can feel something in the air. She inspires and excites you.

We have all tried to be nice. We have tried to fit in. We have tried to be what our parents, teachers, and society told us we should be. We really tried to do what was expected. We have been polite, cordial, agreeable, and smiley. We have gritted our teeth instead of speaking up. We tucked in our opinions and desires. We have been bored and we have been slightly boring. That was before, before we knew better.

We really tried to do what was expected. We have been polite, cordial, agreeable, and smiley. We have gritted our teeth instead of speaking up. We have been bored and we have been slightly boring. That was before, before we knew better.

Not to worry! If you are bored and you know it, there is hope. If you are weary of perfection, duplication, and comparison, there is definitely reason for optimism. The seeds of character are germinating, and with night sweats and hot flashes, you will soon be blooming. "If I can live through hot flashes," Roxie says, "I can live through anything." With a little magic and poetic intention, we can overcome all limiting, half-baked, or tedious tendencies. After menopause, we have more energy and clarity. We come to our senses. Here is a prescription for how:

Take gentle care of your body. A woman of experience is at ease with her body. She knows it's the only one she will ever have. She pays close attention to what her body is craving and makes certain to give herself that. She eats appropriate food. If it's a leafy salad that she wants, she eats that. If Roxie wants a piece of lemon meringue pie, she goes to the nearest bakery, eats one piece, and comes home. She no longer brings it home and eats the whole pie. She takes only what she needs. A woman with pizzazz knows how her body responds to exercise and participates in the physical activities that suit her best. Roxie goes to water aerobics each morning. She appreciates the importance of pampering and touch. Roxie gets massages, manicures, pedicures, and facials. When she is tired, she rests. She may put her feet up or go to bed. She may put on her robe and lounge around all week. No matter what, Roxie speaks kindly about her body. She is way beyond calling herself "too fat" or "too old." She is more interested in feeling comfortable in her own skin than calling her body names.

Accentuate your quirks. A spunky rebel turns her quirks into trademarks. She is unique and she appreciates those qualities that make her one of a kind. She has made peace with her funny, peculiar ways. She is comfortable with each and every one.

If Roxie is in the middle of a particularly creative phase, she will put a clear message on her answering machine, "I'm in retreat and not taking calls. Leave a message and I'll return your call in a month. Love ya."

Our quirks, like fingerprints, define us. A spirited rebel appreciates differences. She does not apologize for or disguise her peculiar or exceptional ways. "You can only be you," Roxie says, "and I can only be me." We can't be anyone else; we are who we are. So relax. Existence needs us just as we are—quirks and all.

Share your genius. A creative rebel is not only comfortable and confident with her abilities and aptitudes, she knows she has a mission to share them. She knows her strengths, and if she doesn't she follows her interests until she finds them again. She recognizes the spark of inspiration and responds. She is courageous about putting forth what she knows. If she feels the urge to write poetry, she does it. She does not apologize if it's not perfect. She doesn't say, "Oh, I can't write poetry." If she has the urge to try, she does. If she needs guidance, she asks. She's committed to enjoying herself in the process. She does not compare her poems to others. She delights in her own limericks, rhymes, and literary sentences. She supports her friends' talents as well. She knows that a friend's poetry does not detract from her own. She has put away the imaginary yardstick and has stopped measuring herself. She accentuates her talents, spreads the good word about other women's genius, and is joyful in the process.

Our second adulthood is magically shaping us into our most original and spunky selves. All our experiences—happy and not so happy—have molded us. They are useful. They have given us depth. Don't worry if your life has been difficult—that alone has turned many boring, nice, nice ladies into rebels with oomph and pizzazz. Remembers, creative characters are made, not born.

To Do or Not to Do

1. Focus. Do you really want to be known as Ms. Too Nice?
2. Explain yourself by saying, "Darling. A girl's gotta do what a girl's gotta do."
3. Think of it this way: "It's not easy to be who you are, but it's more natural than trying to be someone else."
4. Put a message on your answering machine that reflects your artistic persona such as, "I'm writing a novel, can't talk now."
5. Live with pizzazz. Remember, it's hard knocks that turn nice ladies into geniuses.

"For God gives to some of her children a special gift,
which we might call the courage to be mad, to be outside
the mainstream, to live and dance on the edge of life where psyche
and cosmos meet, where Spirit flows into the human, where only
the angels have surefootedness to tread lightly."

—MATTHEW FOX

A Is Not for Aging, A Is for Attitude

> Age doesn't define who we are or who we can become.
> There is no such thing as too much woman.
> With comfy walking shoes, reading glasses, and the right shade of lipstick, anything is possible.
> When youthful beauty fades, it is necessary to use imagination and develop other talents.
> Rejuvenation is a bucket of paint, expensive dark chocolate, and a deep-tissue massage.
> We cannot choose when we are going to die, but we can choose how we are going to live.
> We are part of all things under heaven.

Section Three . . .

Ode to That Darling Stage

You didn't know it then, but you know it for certain now—you don't always get what you think you want. You plan for one thing and you get another. Fortunately, what you get is often better than you could have dreamed. There are perks that come with being softer, gentler, rounder. Love never leaves us alone. It comes when we least expect it, in ways we may never have known before. A mixture of passion and compassion blended with acceptance and gratitude. Love touches us still and grows sweeter.

Beauty in Knowing Who You Are

Middle aged women really do look great! Look around and you will notice that women are looking fabulous. They used to say, "You're not getting older, you're getting better." Evidently we are getting younger too. Newspapers and magazine articles proclaim it:

> *40 is the new 30.*
> *50 is new 40.*
> *60 is the new 50.*

When Oprah turned fifty, she announced that fifty is the new thirty!
Middle age isn't what it used to be when women looked their age. This is encouraging. It means we can get away with more. We can date younger if we want to. We can have babies at almost any age.

We can move our bodies in ways that our grandmothers hadn't even thought of. We can change careers, husbands, houses, and identities, go to the gym, plant a garden, become an artist, and still have time to search for the meaning of life. There is so much freedom in being middle-aged. We can flounder around, be flawed, take time off, and still bounce back. At middle age we have roaming room to figure out how we want to spend four more decades. We have the time, the tools, and the gumption to grow into who we are becoming.

Fifty-one-year-old Bianca is putting the superwoman out to pasture and resigning from being a caretaker. "I do not have to be everything to everybody any longer." Her son and daughter are almost out of the house and she has plans for herself. "I'm excited and I have options." Middle-aged women have oh so many choices. "I'm more secure in myself than ever," Bianca says, "and more mature."

Middle-age years are the decades for being who we are and the age that we are. When we are enjoying ourselves, that glow of confidence is very appealing. We are competent. We are not easily shaken because we know ourselves better. We are not trying to be something that we are not. When we accept ourselves, we radiate self-assurance. We know who we are, and we are not swayed. We are softer, yet stronger. Our energy is high.

Middle age is confidence in who we are and where we're headed. That is always chic. Mackea is creating a blended family with her new husband, his two children, and her two children. His cat is meeting her dog. She is opening a second consignment clothing store, cooking dinner every night, and working out with weights. "Age is not something you need to apologize for," Mackea says. "I don't camouflage it." Three years ago, she let her hair turn gray. "I started turning gray in my twenties, and by thirty-nine I was tired of getting my roots done." She chopped it all off and hasn't colored it since. "I'm OK with gray as long as it is spiky, funky, and messy." According to Mackea, gray hair is a blessing. "I don't mind that young hot guys don't hit on me any longer, because they are so respectful. I get better service and people call me ma'am."

We are over forty. We have been around the block a few times and it shows. We are glad that we look good, but we aren't obsessing over each wrinkle. Beauty is not about perfection. We would rather be authentic than perfect. Middle age elegance is sexy, attractive, desirable, and tender. It is confidence, wisdom, and a spring in the step. It is the jump-up joy that comes with appreciating our real selves that knocks their socks off.

To Do or Not to Do

1. Get away with as much as you can.
2. Smile and be amused when you are called ma'am.
3. Cheer for authentic beauty.
4. Knock their socks off with your aura of confidence.
5. Wear your gray hair choppy and messy.

"An older woman looks good wearing bright red lipstick.
This is not true of younger women or drag queens."

—ANDY ROONEY

Gypsy Souls with Wheels

There is more than one way to get from one place to another. Maybe a zesty car isn't for you, but that doesn't mean that you can't express yourself and get around at the same time. Anne Lise's chosen transportation is a purple, silver, and chrome motorcycle. For Ms. Karen, it's a pearly white Vespa, and for me (known as LilyD when I am wearing

my artsy, wild woman persona), it's a Euro-looking electric bike with
a basket on the front. The three of us are very different, but we are all
intriguing in our own right. In my younger, more insecure decades, I
might have gotten wrapped up in comparing myself to them, but now
I'm too busy seeing clients, writing, painting walls or canvas, and riding my bike. With so much going on, I don't have the energy to beat
myself up, put myself down, or improve on myself the way I did when
I was twenty and thirty.

 Our primary task of raising children has ended, which means we can
ride into uncharted territory and discover something new.

Perhaps it is wanderlust in our veins that compels us to take to the
road. Perhaps it is the liberation that comes with an empty nest. Our
primary task of raising children has ended, which means we can ride
into uncharted territory and discover something new. Without the
daily task of driving children to their activities, we have roaming room
to meander through eclectic neighborhoods, to explore what is over
the horizon, to imbibe in the freedom of fresh air blowing through our
hair. Anne Lise bought her first Harley at fifty-three and now, at fifty-
nine, she's on her third. She's always been a wild woman, always had
that undomesticated drive, and since her three children are raised, she
can take to the road without all that motherly guilt tagging along. Ms.
Karen, on the other hand, was and still is quite refined. It wasn't until a
bout of skin cancer cracked her very proper veneer that she took to the
road. Her sweet husband bought her the Vespa after she got the diagnosis and she's been riding and traveling ever since. Me, well, I spent
several years fantasizing about a motorcycle. My friends even gave me
a Harley T-shirt for my fortieth birthday and I wrote an ad: "Ample

Momma with a gypsy soul seeks man on a Harley and/or a gourmet cook. Send picture of hog and/or favorite recipe." I never placed the ad, I never bought the Harley, but I did get my electric bike, which I absolutely adore. I'm a free spirit on that bike, riding to the farmer's markets on the weekend. Filling the basket with flowers and French bread, I fancy myself Parisian. As I ride along the shores of Lake Washington, I pretend that I'm an artist living in Paris. I love those beautiful old bridges over the Seine River. Many famous artists have painted that river. Can't you just see me carrying brushes and paints in my basket? I am ecstatic to be smack in the middle of my freedom years. I can hop on my bike and go anywhere. Riding around wearing a colorful scarf around my neck, just like the ladies of Paris, I am as playful as a child again, free of worries and full of imagination.

Anne Lise says she'll do anything once. Something starts vibrating within her and she just has to follow it. Like sleeping in the jungle in Fiji or jumping out of a plane or scuba diving with sharks. She has to challenge all her fears. Once on a ride from Phoenix to the annual motorcycle rally in Sturgis, South Dakota, she noticed a guy in a truck circling around her while she was pitching her tent. She thought to herself, "Am I supposed to be scared?" and then she decided, "Well, if I'm supposed to be scared, I'd rather know my enemy." She waved the guy over and made a point of talking to him. He ended up parking his truck next to her tent, and they had breakfast together the next morning before she rode off. The next day she rode into Sturgis with the Bandidos motorcycle gang that she'd met on the highway. It was raining all day and her 850-pound bike with 150 pounds of gear on the back got stuck in three feet of mud, and it was the big hairy Hell's Angel that came to her rescue. Anne Lise says the bikers take care of her, and I imagine it has something to do with her long, fluffy white hair and open heart. She says she used to be judgmental about bikers, but not since she was up close and personal with 90,000 of them at the rally.

Ms. Karen is challenging her fears, too. The pearly white Vespa is a reminder that she has lots of living to do. Cancer is a teacher, she says, and she's not going to let fear hold her back anymore. Her day-to-day routine hasn't changed much, but on the inside she feels freer and this summer she's going with her husband on a Vespa Club ride through Oregon. Her daughter can't believe that very same mom who wouldn't ever be seen without a full face of makeup is willing to put on a helmet and smash her hair. Just goes to show that our kids don't know all our sides.

As youngsters, Anne Lise's kids wished for a mother like all the other kids had. Now she says they appreciate that she had guts to be different because they're finding the guts to be different, too. My kid used to say something similar to me. "Mom," she said, "you're crazy, but it's a good crazy." She still says it and I take it as a compliment.

We three ladies like our wheels—they are part of our personalities. The great thing about middlescence is that the longer you are middleaged, the less you are bound by dogmas and rigid standards of "acceptable" behavior. Anne Lise says her desires for life are always bigger than her pocketbook. She either had to give up her lifestyle or give up her house, so she sold her house. Ms. Karen and I admire her wanderlust courage, but we're the exact opposites. We're homebodies. Our home is our temple and our sanctuary. We find adventures in other ways. "Viva la difference!" we say. We don't have it all figured out and perhaps that's what Anne Lise means when she says, "The soul is always searching, always hungry." I guess that's why we ride—we ride to comfort our gypsy soul.

To Do or Not to Do

1. Admit it! You've got a wild side.
2. List three wild things that you'd be willing to do once.
3. Challenge your fears by making friends with the enemy.
4. Take a wild ride. Call up your local Harley dealer and ask someone to take you out for a ride. If Harleys don't speak to you, try a Honda, rent a Vespa, or check out a chic electric bike.
5. Christen yourself with a wild name to match your gypsy soul.

"Laugh and the world laughs with you.
Cry and you cry with your girlfriends."

—Laurie Kuslansky

Inspired Second Chances

Lola reads cookbooks for fun, clips recipes from magazines, makes up her own concoctions, and organizes them on her computer. She's resigned, however, from the daily chore of cooking. She prefers being served now, so she either eats out; picks up from the deli; or Hank, her hubby, cooks one of his favorites. Just because she reads recipes doesn't mean she has to cook. She's been there, done that, for her family of four. The kids moved out, Lola is moving on, and Hank is developing his chef persona. Lola is still a foodie, but with a fresh angle. Her intention is to incorporate recipes into a book that she's writing about resigning from cooking. Isn't she inventive? She's putting a creative spin on what she enjoys. It's not something she has to do, it's something that she wants to do. Second chances are so much sweeter than first chances.

The second half of life is a silver platter of second chances.

The second half of life is a silver platter of second chances. Here's a second chance to go beyond attaining it all, to embracing it all. Here's a chance to stretch beyond perfection. The first half of life is striving for perfection in all forms. The second half is pure improvisation. Instead of being bogged down by obligations, we're bouncing up with possibilities. Here is another chance to play, go wild, create, soul search, soak up blessings, do what you love, and love unconditionally.

That is what Jasmine is doing. She switched from full-time retail career to part-time in order to strike out on her own. She's combining her retail experience with her fascination for sewing ribbons on T-shirts and designing the hottest workout shirts around. She planned to sell them at the outdoor Saturday market, but when she and a girlfriend wore bright orange ribbons sewn on hot pink shirts to the aerobics class, Jasmine got so many orders that she hasn't been able to build up an inventory yet. Her tiny success is huge because it's given a boost to her career. "I don't think I will ever retire now that I can combine work with play." Her retail expertise, fashion sense, and dream to design have—like pieces of a puzzle—finally come together.

Inspired second chances belong to the realm of the miraculous. Forty-eight-year-old Cynthia is living her artistic dream as a photographer. She always has, but she didn't always know it. That's true for many of us. We don't know how our experiences will fit together until we live long enough to look back. We don't realize how well our endeavors work out until twenty or thirty years later, when we look back and see how all those years and ventures came together. When you're in your thirties and not even working in your field, let alone being recognized, it's not always clear where you're heading. Sometimes you feel hopelessly off course. "Am I deluding myself?" you wonder. "Will I ever be an artist?"

Then, like Cynthia, you sell your first creation to someone other than a family member. You decide it's a fluke and doubt that you'll sell another one again. When a complete stranger offers to buy one of your pieces, it gives you a boost that others appreciate your work, too. That's why Cynthia's beginning to accept that she's a real-life, working, bona fide photographer. With gallery shows and exhibitions on her resume, with strangers buying her pieces, she's claiming her title and coming into her own. "I always wanted the artistic lifestyle," she says, "I never, ever wanted a regular job, I never wanted to be a dental hygienist." Cynthia never was a dental hygienist, but she did work in the corporate world, which, for her at the time, seemed far from her dream of making a living as a photographer. After ten years in the corporate world, Cynthia retired with enough jingle in her pocket to pursue her artistic dream. "Once I got my hands into Dektol again, I was hooked." Photography is solitary and she wondered if she was detaching from the world. "But really taking pictures focuses me on the world, I'm really looking, really seeing." Through the eyes of a photographer, Cynthia notices oddities, nuances, and ironies, things she might not notice without a camera.

That's the miracle of midlife. We're able to understand how where we have been got us to where we were going. We're able see things from a broader perspective. We have lived long enough to know that our life is a work in progress, that one step leads to another, and that the Almighty always gives us more chances.

To Do or Not to Do

1. Give yourself a silver platter and serve up second chances.
2. Buy an unlined spiral notebook. (I like spiral notebooks because you can lay them flat while writing or pasting.) This will be your "Inspired Second Chance Journal." It's an illustrated manuscript of second chance dreams. Written by you, for you, about you, and dedicated to you.

3. Look at the world as a photographer might; see all the angles.
4. Paste a collage of pictures in a journal and write a few sentences about them. Include your favorite recipes.
5. Improvise and let yourself be served.

*"A woman is like a tea bag. You never know how
strong she is until she gets into hot water."*

—Eleanor Roosevelt

From Drama Queen to Wise Woman

Stella is a self-proclaimed drama queen, always was and still is. But in recent years, she's grown wiser about how she expresses that side of herself. In her twenties, she was addicted to butterflies in the stomach, soap operas, and conflict. She was demanding. She was needy and needed to be adored. She ran after romance and fell in love with being in love. She was sexy. She was dizzy. She was up and then she was down. She was melodramatic.

She met Henry in a college theater. It was the perfect stage romance. She had the lead role and he was the director. Stella expected a storybook ending. But she was in a hurry, a competition, a contest to get married and make babies. She and Henry promised "love you forever" when they wrote their vows. She thought that a promise was all that was needed. "I knew that relationships were hard work, but I didn't find out what that meant until it was almost too late." By the end of her twenties, she'd gone through a quarterlife crisis. Stella wanted a child, but Henry was ambivalent. She pleaded and he stalled. She finally got her way and stayed home to care for two toddlers. But before long, she began to suffer from angst and housewife syndrome. She played tennis and was a top-notch volunteer for children's causes. Henry went to work and earned so much money that he couldn't change careers even though he sometimes yearned to. By then, the family was used to a certain standard of living.

They became preoccupied with the mundane tasks of married and family life. They stopped talking about their dreams. Communication and sex drifted to the back burner and eventually off the stove. Stella was depressed and Henry was putting in long hours.

When the kids started junior high, Stella had an awakening. She was living on the edge of "I know everything about you" boredom with Henry. When both her brother's and sister's marriages fell apart, Stella woke up. She read a book about what it takes to keep marriages thriving. She cared for Henry and he for her, but the connection between them was lukewarm. They saw a marriage counselor. They fought it out, cried it out, talked it out, and gained fresh insights. Their discoveries brought them closer. And they went back to the beginning—they went back to the theater. "When Henry and I thought we could no longer live together, when we had nothing to say to each other, when we were wounded, it was returning to the theater and acting classes that brought us back together."

We've all been disillusioned by love. We forget why we fell for each other in the first place. Romance withers and intimacy slips away as the demands of daily life take over. We fall out of love and into routine. It's a staggering dilemma. How does one stay emotionally connected while raising a family and building a nest egg? Minor disappointments can blow up to tragic proportions. Our intentions may be good, but our follow-through is slacking. When our relationship is tested, we blame each other instead of looking for the real answer.

Love is not perfect and Stella has learned not to expect it to be. That is the wisdom she's gained. We are all vulnerable. Our partners are human. With a little wisdom under our belts we learn to dust ourselves off, apologize for our flaws and missteps, and bow to the mystery that can't be described. We open our hearts because it feels better than closing off or withdrawing. We stop trying to change each other. We are less in love with fantasy and more in love with an ordinary human being. We find comfort in each other's presence.

> "Love is growing sweeter and deeper than I thought it could be," Stella told me. "It's not the lust or longing or desperation of my twenties and thirties, it's much kinder than that."

Stella and Henry joined community theater. "Love is growing sweeter and deeper than I thought it could be," Stella told me. "It's not the lust or longing or desperation of my twenties and thirties, it's much kinder than that." Stella is still dramatic—only now instead of getting depressed and fighting with Henry, she channels that energy into the characters she portrays. "I still have a drama queen in me," she admits, "but I'm becoming a wise woman, too."

To Do or Not to Do

1. Keep tabs on the emotional temperature of your relationship. If it's lukewarm, you'd better warm it up quickly.
2. Write a love letter to your sweetheart. Describe a time when you truly felt connected.
3. Apologize. An apology is the quickest healer.
4. Indulge in the dramatic. Try acting classes as therapy.
5. Keep the little drama queen around for entertainment now and then. Be wise about how you use her.

"There's nothing like a good heartbreak to get a good song."

—K.D. LANG

We've Got Spirit

The world would be really boring without women. Without us, there would be no celebrations, no birthday parties, no holiday dinners, no presents, no decorations, and no embellishment. There would be no ambiance. Everything would be tedious, lackluster, and terribly dull. Think about it. It's women who turn office routines into parties, it's women who wrap the presents, it's women who put "love you" notes in lunchboxes, it's women who orchestrate the social calendar.

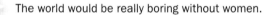

The world would be really boring without women.

Women's imaginations are as big as the sky. They are creative geniuses! They sew fringe on lampshades and ruffles on pillows. Natalie bought mismatched china at the flea market—from a lady who makes soap in her basement—and gave it to her niece as a wedding present. Mia inherited her grandmother's vintage button and bead collection, and instead of keeping them in boxes, she sews them with ribbons onto leather and turns them into bracelets.

Brooke bought six broken-down bar stools at a garage sale, decoupaged the legs and arms, reupholstered the seats, and when she was finished donated them to the high school auction. Those stools raised more money for senior prom than the trip—donated by the automobile dealerships—for two to Las Vegas. See what I mean about genius?

We often think of a creative genius as an unusual intelligence or a brilliant mind. But the original meaning of the word *genius* is an attendant spirit of a person, a person who is a positive influence on another. That certainly describes the women I know and I'm fairly certain that if you think about it, you too are a positive influence on others. If you've baked a cake and shared it with a neighbor, if you've cut roses from your garden and arranged them into a bouquet, if you've knitted a scarf and given it away, you know the pure pleasure that comes when you share what you've created.

We often think of a creative genius as an unusual intelligence or a brilliant mind. But the original meaning of the word *genius* is an attendant spirit of a person, a person who is a positive influence on another.

Creativity is intoxicating, it's joy infused with a little frustration and Ingrid knows about frustration. She bakes and decorates cakes. "I'm an apprentice," she tells me as she pulls the little cakes out of the oven. She took a cake decorating class and has become obsessed with perfecting pansies and daffodils that she molds from sweet icing. When I referred to her cupcakes, she corrected me, "Not cupcakes, little cakes." The day I visited her, she had thirty-six cooling on the counter and four iced. Only one little cake had passed her inspection and gone to the "save for the party" pile. The other three were in the "OK to eat now" pile. Ingrid knows exactly how she wants them to look, and if they don't meet her standards, she lets you eat them right away. "The most important thing is to love what you're creating."

Women are the memory makers, the storytellers, and the tradition keepers. Women tell stories about the neighbors, the relatives, and people they've never even met. They paste pictures of babies and families in scrapbooks. They are the backbone of inspiration and genius at getting done whatever needs to be done. "Creatively conjuring up something out of nothing is what women do," Ingrid says, "and I'm passionate about little cakes."

As long as we continue to conjure the creative energy in ourselves, we are making a contribution, leaving our mark, discovering our own little cakes.

To Do or Not to Do

1. Use your imagination. Pick one boring routine, such as doing the laundry, and turn it into a party. I don't know how you can do that, but you'll figure it out.
2. Spruce things up. Sew fringe on lampshades, tassels on curtains, ruffles on pillows, and beads on pants.
3. Buy a chair from a flea market and decoupage it. Donate it to a fundraiser.
4. Bake a couple little cakes. Give one to the neighbor and eat one.
5. Get some pompoms. Give a spirited cheer for spirited women.

"If you have a burning restless urge to write or paint, simply eat something sweet and the feeling will pass."

—Fran Lebowitz

𝒟ℴ 𝒥𝓉 𝓌𝒾𝓉𝒽 𝒻𝓁𝒶𝒾𝓇 . . .

> Almost always drink from goblets.
> Almost always eat by candlelight.
> Almost always use a tablecloth on a picnic.
> Almost always keep the refrigerator clean.
> Almost always swim in the nude.
> Almost always tell the truth.
> Almost always cook with herbs.
> Almost always ruffle a few feathers.
> Almost never follow advice.

Relationship Troubles

The year Julia turned forty-nine her husband tearfully confessed to having an affair with the thirty-one-year-old receptionist at his office. The details were comparable to cases we've all heard about—older wealthy man gives gifts and trips in exchange for feeling young again. The betrayal was like being hit in the stomach with a two-by-four, and it took a month or more for Julia to catch her breath. Charlie begged her to stay and promised to do whatever it took. Still, it took several years to untangle the mess.

Some years are bleaker than others are, and for Julia her forty-ninth year was grueling. Should she stay? Should she go? Could she forgive him, trust him, let him back in her bed? Important questions for sure, but insignificant in comparison to the big ones that plagued her daily. Why did she feel partially responsible for what had happened? Why should she? After all, she hadn't been unfaithful. Why couldn't she simply point the finger, blame him, and be done? Meaningful questions that even her clergy couldn't answer. "Walk away, get a divorce," she told herself often. That's what others did when they

had caught a husband cheating. "But if I go, the questions go with me."
And so while she searched for her answers she stayed. "I have one foot
in our marriage and one foot on the dock," she told Charlie. Within her,
however, was an ember of hope.

There are questions that no one—except ourselves—can answer.

There are questions that no one—except ourselves—can answer.
The best that anyone else can do for us is to point in the directions where
the answers might be found. Julia wasn't sure if or how she'd contrib-
uted to the stress her relationship was in, but she wondered if, in some
way, she had. To blame him would be easy; to take responsibility for her
part was beyond comprehension. She didn't know if she had it in her.

Thus began Julia's long search to sort through confusion, to
rebuild her relationship or leave? On her fiftieth birthday, she and
Charlie made a formal commitment. In the presence of a few friends,
they pledged to make changes in the way they communicate and relate
so that they both could be happy. "I care enough about you," they
said out loud, "to work out the kinks in our relationship. I promise to
consider carefully my contribution to the trouble we've been having."
After the brief ceremony, they all went out dancing and they've been
dancing a lot since. Dancing, they agree, balances out the intensity of
their discussions.

No doubt about it, long-term relationships face challenges, too.
Julia shared with me five answers that she found that might point the
way for you if you ever have your own relationship trials.

1. It's natural to want to turn your back on someone who has
   betrayed you.

2. It's not wise to strike back while you're feeling humiliated and bruised.
3. A relationship needs breathing room, but avoiding each other builds higher walls between you.
4. You don't have to be absolutely sure.
5. One small change can make a world of difference.

When Julia turned fifty-one, she wanted a little breathing room and Charlie agreed to her plan. She took her best girlfriend on an ultra-luxurious safari and Charlie picked up the tab. It felt good that she could once again trust enough to leave him and he felt good knowing that he was once again trustworthy. It is easy to love someone who is perfect, but to love someone who has disappointed us and let us down, well, that's a love to notice.

To Do or Not to Do

1. Take a relationship inventory. How are you and your sweetheart doing?
2. Search for your own answers. Let others point the way, but know that no two couples are alike.
3. Take your share of the responsibility for any distress that your relationship is in.
4. Fire up your inner Tarzan and Jane. Go on an ultraluxurious safari—no matter what's going on in your relationship, camping in style with lions and giraffes roaming around will add spark.
5. Show tenderness to yourself and your honey.

"Within a love relationship there are many endings."

—Dr. Clarissa Pinkola Estés

Midlife Momma

Forty-nine-year-old Cynthia has no trouble falling asleep. With four-year-old twins to run after all day long, she's exhausted and happy. Thirty minutes after her four-year-old twins are in bed, she's hit the sack and is dreaming. Cynthia had hoped to have her children earlier, but that's not how it all came together. "Dating, finding the right man, getting married, and having kids," she says, "is like fixing Thanksgiving dinner. It seldom comes out at the exact time like you plan it." Whether it's marriage and children or giblets and gravy, it's almost impossible to master the timing so that everything is ready when you'd like it.

> "Dating, finding the right man, getting married, and having kids is like fixing Thanksgiving dinner. It seldom comes out at the exact time like you plan it."

Cynthia wanted to get married after college but the guys she was seeing just wanted to date. She was frustrated that she hadn't found the right guy and felt too old to become a nun, like her sister had. "I was beginning to wonder what God was saving me for," Cynthia remembers. Though her relationships with men weren't going as she'd planned, her friendships with women were nurturing and stable. In her more insecure moments, Cynthia wondered, "Are you born a lesbian or can you become one?" Since being alone is preferable to being with the wrong guy, she amused herself for years with work and travel.

The universe works in mysterious ways and Jack, who is nine-and-a-half years younger than Cynthia, came on the scene when she was thirty-five. "When you find the right one it's so easy to be together," she says, "but I wanted to make sure he was serious." She was up front with Jack, and told him that if he expected dinner on the table at five o'clock every night, he shouldn't marry her. Besides, she was dragging her feet because she liked being single.

Jack convinced her that he didn't expect dinner, and at thirty-seven she agreed to marry him. "I married my babysitter," Jack proudly teases. A year later they were ready for a baby. "I should have studied fertility in college instead of sociology," she says. "There was so much about my body that I didn't know." "Let's don't put pressure on ourselves," Jack said. "I'll be happy with you, with or without children." Finally, after two miscarriages, two exploratory surgeries, and in vitro fertilization, at age forty-five Cynthia was expecting.

There's always more to learn about a body. At thirty-nine-and-a-half weeks along, Cynthia was eager for labor. Her body was swollen, the babies were kicking, and Jack wanted to fool around a little. Cynthia was too big and inflated to romp and roll or even cuddle. She had heard, however, that sexual activity might induce labor so she was willing to give it a try. She did not go into the details, but she did tell the members of her book club that her water broke precisely at his most critical moment. Isn't that a novel approach to labor?

The twins were born twenty-two hours later, weighing six pounds, four ounces, and six pounds, six ounces. Isn't it amazing how determination, imagination, and trusting our urges can deliver the goods? Whether it's Thanksgiving dinner, finding the right man, or having babies, the age of the cook or mother doesn't matter, it's that you enjoy the process and stay with it. Midlife mommas have many options. They know that they can cook or not cook, they can marry younger, and they can have babies. Age has nothing to do with cooking, marrying, sex, or loving children. Age does not limit the potential, abilities, or genius of a woman.

To Do or Not to Do

1. If you're tossing and turning all night, borrow someone's four-year-old twins and take care of them for a week.

2. Trust your body and learn how it functions.

3. Open up. Really talk to your book club. Be uninhibited and set the example. Invite each member to share.

4. If you are expecting, overdue, and eager for labor, try the novel approach and fool around a little. That might do the trick.

5. If you're unmarried, consider exploring the pleasures of a younger guy, but tell him clearly not to expect dinner.

"When you are as old as I you will know there is only one thing in the world worth living for, and that is sin."

—LADY SPERANZA WILDE

Still Pretty As a Picture

Have you ever stumbled across a picture of yourself from long ago and been surprised at what you saw? You wonder how the girl in the picture can possibly be you. Perhaps you were prettier and thinner than you remembered. Perhaps your smile reminds you of a different time in your life—a time when you were naïve, when you were a little cocky, when you were sure the world had a big secret to tell you.

It was a twenty-year-old album that captured the attention of forty-four-year-old Jade. She was familiar with all the pictures, she had seen them countless times before, but this time when she looked at the images she noticed her shining hair, her svelte body, her eyes, and her energetic spirit, characteristics that she so often dismissed in herself as a young woman. Seeing herself in those photos took her back.

She was twenty-two and living in an apartment with two roommates. It was Sunday morning and the three of them were up at the crack of dawn, cooking breakfast and getting ready to run the Boston Marathon. They were pumped up, taking pictures of each other, smiling, and giving thumbs up. Jade, her dark hair in a ponytail, her blue running shorts and top perfectly matched to her eyes, was stretching against the counter. Jade had always liked that picture and seeing it brought back many fond memories of that carefree year in the city. But it also brought some sadness. At twenty-two she was a vibrant, feminine, lively spirit with a healthy, beautiful body. "Why couldn't I see it then?" she wondered. "Why was I so critical about my thighs, why had I called myself a fat pig?" Looking at the pictures was an epiphany. Her body image was distorted. "I wasn't ugly or fat," she thought. "I wish I would have known how fresh and beautiful I really was because I could have treated myself much nicer."

We've all done it—degraded our thighs, poked fun at our hips, and hid our upper arms. Our poor little bodies have endured such verbal abuse. We imagine that our nose is too big and our midriff too thick. At every stage we find something that doesn't suit us, our chin, our skin, our hair. If we have curly hair we wish it could be straighter, if it's straight we envy natural curls. We have insecurities and judgments about every body part. Our breasts are never the right size. They are either too big or too small. We walk past a mirror or a window and we can barely look at our reflection, sometimes we call ourselves names. We've all been ferocious about weight.

Many of us don't begin to appreciate our bodies until we're in our middle years. That's when we notice how beautiful young women are. We realize that we were once like the lovely young women we see all around us; we only wish we would have known it when we were twenty. We appreciate their exuberance and we wish we would have been more confident about our looks. We don't see our loveliness until we're looking back. "I am going to enjoy my body and appreciate my looks," Jade decided. "I don't want to be seventy looking back at fifty wishing I would have been nicer to myself."

In midlife, we have a second chance to give up hating our bodies. This tendency to feel ashamed if we aren't perfect or thin is a national obsession. It's time to turn it around. We can make a change. By seeing ourselves clearly, we can start the revolution and spread the word.

To Do or Not to Do

1. Compliment body parts. Say something nice every day about your waist, hips, and thighs.
2. Be pleased with your breasts. It's not size that matters, it's that you have them.
3. Applaud femininity. Those lines are ruffles, not wrinkles.
4. Spread admiration freely. Give compliments away.
5. Look through old photographs. See how pretty you were then and see how pretty you are now.

"Oh God, help me to see the truth about myself
no matter how beautiful it is."

—ANONYMOUS

Creative Napping

I'm a gourmet napper. I nap the way a foodie eats—relishing every moment. Naps in the late afternoon are the most luxurious for me. I get some of my best ideas curled up underneath my comforter. A couple of summers ago, I moved an antique iron twin bed outdoors, and there, wrapped in a slice of sunlight, I find a sanctuary in which my joints and muscles untighten and I'm free to dream, to create. When I

get writer's phobia or if I'm suffering from "I can't think of a
write" panic, my outdoor bedroom becomes my refuge. Dur
winter months, I curl up in front of the fire.

Napping is the artistic side of sleeping. That's why when I'm in a
creative mood, I don't worry about taking my first catnap around 10
A.M. Since I get up at 5 A.M., I'm ready for a rest by then. I get my worst
ideas when I am tired, so sleep is divinely refreshing. Pressure to perform melts away with a nap, and fresh inspirations are more likely to
bubble up. I keep my journal close by so I can write down any brilliant
gems that come to me. Even if I don't fall asleep, just lying down, closing my eyes, and being silent is enough of a change of pace that I am
able to think more clearly when I do go back to writing. The biggest
enemy to writing is not paying attention when my body is screaming
for a nap. When I am on a creative roll, the permission to rest that
I have granted myself keeps me positive and sometimes writing past
midnight.

Creative naps are idea-generators for many women. Salle, a children's writer-to-be, begins her nap by closing the door to her tiny 8
foot by 6 foot writing studio and hanging her "Siesta Time" sign on the
doorknob. Alone in her studio, she withdraws from the demands of
being a wife and mother. For Salle, her writing studio is a way to stay
connected to her creativity. When she feels guilty about saying no to
family and friends, guilty about withdrawing, she reminds herself that
she's got to stay true to her dreams. She stands firm in her conviction
that she's a writer. If she gets sidetracked and doesn't take care of her
need for creative time, she ends up feeling out of sorts.

Blocks are an instructive feeling that we have been pushing ourselves too hard. If we feel stuck on a creative project, we can take a
break instead of straining for an idea; we can shift to a slower pace,
and then the ideas seem to come effortlessly. It is out of that easy, open

space that we are most often inspired. Instead of pushing through our creative walls, it's wiser to accept the inertia as a message. "During my siesta, I often come upon a beautiful phrase, a lovelier word, a livelier line," Salle says. "If I get out of my own way, my unconscious does the work for me." In that crucial moment before slipping into slumber, she specifically opens to guidance about the children's book that she's working on. "I need help," she says to herself, and then instead of ruminating about her lack of creativity, she thinks, "I know it will come." Rest is a conduit from one creator to the universal creator, from which all ideas flow. When her mind is frozen, Salle knows better than to bulldoze her way through, and this is a lesson that all of us can learn from. "When I wake up, I may not have a complete idea or even a phrase, but I have a clearer direction of where I'm going with the project."

All creative types need down time—stretches of space to do nothing, to reflect and be calm. Time to recuperate, unwind, and refresh. We're all so used to running and rushing that when we have free time, we often feel restless and fidgety instead of taking a moment to relax.

The clearest ideas float down when we stand still long enough to catch them.

The clearest ideas float down when we stand still long enough to catch them. My favorite tarot reader, Ms. Zenith, calls that channeling. Whatever you call it—napping, a siesta, channeling, time out, or unblocking, it really doesn't matter. What matters is that by withdrawing from what is expected of us, we allow the artistic juices to flow again. Artists in the fine and messy art of living know, you can't force genius, you have to take a nap and receive it.

To Do or Not to Do

1. Choose a place other than your bedroom for a creative nap.
2. Hang out the "Shh! Artist Napping" sign. If you don't have such a sign, make one.
3. Stand still. Stand still long enough to catch or to channel all the fresh ideas floating around. Bulldozers push, artists allow.
4. Surrender to resting. Practice receiving. Do it for one week and see what happens.

"In order to hear your calling and answer it, you must generously give yourself the gift of time. It's not how fast you make your dream come true, but how steadily you pursue it."

—Sarah Ban Breathnach

Second-Hand Roses

It's wonderful to tell girlie-girl stories. It really is. Remember those ballerina shoes, tiaras, bangle bracelets, and petticoats that we wore in our girlhoods? If you've kept any items from your childhood, don't just keep them in a box! These items are valuable. They contain your history. They are bridges to your memories. Pull them out and use them as vintage accoutrements around the house.

Just last year, I rescued three dresses from the farthest corner of my closet and hung them on doors in my house. I wore the blue chiffon with the matching four-inch cummerbund to the 1962 Nampa High School prom. Gary Taylor took me to that dance in his blue and white '56 Chevy. I bought that blue dress to match his blue car. Maybe that's the reason he kissed me goodnight. It was his first kiss, but not mine. I'm certain that it was his first kiss because he was shaking so hard that I thought he was having a seizure. That blue dress now hangs over the door in my bedroom. I wonder if Gary ever thinks of me. I wonder what he did with his car.

A knee-length red satin and velvet dress hangs in the guest room and is a perfect match for the red silk comforter on the bed. Looking at that dress melts my heart. It's very sentimental because I wore that dress to a Valentine's Day dance with my husband-to-be, Jack. "You've got the cutest little waist," he told me, and I can tell by looking at that dress that it was true, even though I didn't appreciate it at the time. Wish my waist still measured 22 inches.

A yellow satin cocktail dress with a chiffon overskirt and satin belt hangs in my office next to the picture of Jack and me at our college graduation dance. When I took the dress to the cleaners, the two ladies behind the counter were so shocked. "Can you get these stains out?" I asked. "How long have they been there?" they inquired. "Since my 1966 college graduation," I answered. "What?" They couldn't believe it, they were stunned.

If you don't have dresses, there are probably plenty of other items ready for rejuvenation. Look in your jewelry box. Do you have big, bold jewelry in there that you don't wear anymore? Pull all that costume jewelry out and drape it over vases. Do you have any chunky pins? Use them as napkin rings. Ethnic bracelets, necklaces, and earrings make colorful centerpieces. They look great around doorknobs or hung from lamps. They make great conversation starters.

> There is absolutely no reason why the special belongings from your past can't come out of hiding to be noticed and talked about.

There is absolutely no reason why the special belongings from your past can't come out of hiding to be noticed and talked about. Just because they are out of style doesn't mean they're not useful or beautiful. They are brimming with your history. A clear vase on my dining room table holds pearl necklaces that belonged to my great-aunts and grandmother. They hold stories and meaning. When I entertain, someone usually asks, "Judy, what are those pearl necklaces doing in that vase?" "Oh, it's a long story," I say. Well, you can imagine what happens then. They coax me into telling it. It's a wonderful way to walk down memory lane and share parts of myself with my friends.

I like reminiscing, and so I'm bringing my girlie stuff out of trunks and boxes. It's fun to find a new purpose for the silver bangle bracelets that I wore in college. Right now I am hanging them from a lamp shade. The silver beaded handbag that my aunt gave me looks darling hanging by the light switch in the hallway. We are never too old to be a girlie-girl and besides, have you noticed the styles lately? Look closely and you will see that some of your girlie stuff is back in style and worth a fortune.

To Do or Not to Do

1. Hang old clothing on the wall as art.
2. Bring out vintage apparel, drape it over a chair, and consider it revolving objects of art.
3. Open a shoe museum.
4. Recycle old purses and jewelry. Display them on tables.
5. Accentuate your girlie-girl tendencies. Wear a sentimental piece of jewelry, revamp a coat, or carry an old purse. Check out the latest styles and you will probably find that these items are back in fashion.

"Style is a unique thing. Mine is made up of infinite thoughts and influences gathered over many years."

—PATIENCE BREWSTER

eativity First

> Begin each day with inspiring thoughts and a glass of water.
> Focus on what you know; ask questions about what you don't.
> Nurture what you love, find a lesson in what you hate.
> Master one itsy bitsy step at a time.
> Hang out with artistic types.
> Spend one day in silence.
> Save housework for the end of the day.

Section Four...

CREATIVITY
Is a Miraculous Matter

There's an artist, a creative force, and a capacity for genius rippling within all of us, no matter what medium we choose. We can tap in to our unique form of artistic expression at any moment, and in the second half of life, these creative juices are overflowing. We've all known times when life was very, very grim, and while we've all experienced despair that shatters our hopes, still we find it all fabulously alluring. We were born to arrange sorrow into happiness, to spin senselessness into silliness, and transform tears into joy. These are magical transformations. Miracles! Look closely and you will see that there is a little miracle maker in all of us.

Artist-in-Residence

It is an over-the-top delight to call ourselves artists. As artists, we can bring out our more interesting sides. We can be flamboyant, original, and perhaps even flashy. We can express ourselves and call it art. The only person we are totally compatible with is ourselves. Laughing about our peculiarities and appreciating our multiple-personality self is the highest art form. Finding out what inspires, moves, and soothes us is art. We have to know ourselves to express ourselves, and with so many corners to our personalities, we have an abundance of quirks to share. That is the dividend of being artists—we don't have to be consistent. We can change our personality on a whim. We can write a poem on Monday, tap dance on Tuesday, arrange flowers on Wednesday, rearrange furniture on Thursday, paint nudes on Friday, paint the ceilings on Saturday, and sing in the choir on Sunday. The following week, when our bones are aching, we can take Epson salt baths and lounge. We can dress to match the occasion.

Finding out what inspires, moves, and soothes us is art.

At midlife we can finally decide who we are. We can work at living or play at living. We can be sober and sad or happy and glad. We can be sullen and moody. We can be silly and make a difference. We don't have to take ourselves seriously, but we can be earnest about what we know. When we let go of our rigid ideas of how things are supposed to be, we free ourselves up to explore all aspects of ourselves. If our fantasies are better than our real life, we still have time to live out those fantasies. What is your fantasy?

Nina is an artist, although she doesn't necessarily describe herself that way. Nina's husband hung an "Artist-in-Residence" sign over the front door. He wanted to acknowledge Nina's dedication to her work. She had thought that winning an award or making a sale would be what qualified her to call herself an artist. So far, she hasn't had a show or sold a piece, but she paints nearly every day. She hasn't sold a painting, but that is not the point. She's committed to painting and she's currently working on a series called "Women." Nina went through a phase of painting women in the kitchen, then it was women in the garden, now she is painting women doing a wide range of chores, from sweeping to setting the table.

Nina hasn't had any recognition for her work, but that doesn't bother her. Her friends encourage her to have a gallery show, but Nina isn't focused on that. She is focused on her work. To Nina, painting is desire and it is that desire that is the measure of an artist. Being an artist is being a little reckless, working at it, doing it again and again. Art is discovering an aspect of ourselves and giving it form. Being an artist is the desire to keep doing it again and again.

To Do or Not to Do

1. Hang an "Artist-in-Residence" sign over your front door.
2. Remember, the definition of a successful artist is the desire and ability to keep making art.
3. Keep doing the work. Keep doing the work.
4. Count your personalities and let them out. Express your quirks in any way you can think of.
5. List your fantasies and express them in your art.

"Be yourself. The world worships the original."

—Jean Cocteau

Expression Is Good for the Walls and Your Soul

Fifty-seven-year-old Claire adores color—lots of it. She adorns her white walls with colorful wall-size canvases. Lime green paintings in the hallway, four variegated shades of green in the living room, blue-green in the dining room, yellow and orange in the kitchen, and off-white in her bedroom. The last time that I visited Claire, she was painting two five-foot canvases for her daughter's apartment.

Claire learned to express herself on canvas after the death of her husband, when she was forced to sell the large family house in which they had lived. Since she couldn't paint the walls in her rented apartment, she turned on her creativity to make the rented space her own. She painted her first canvas two shades of green and hung it in her living room.

Claire never considered herself an artist and until then, she'd never painted on canvas. But by taking the chance, she learned something new about herself.

"Where do you buy such large paintings?" ask the women who visit her home. Claire's friends are amazed that she could take such a big chance. Many of them say, "Oh, I wish I could do that."

"You can," is Claire's response. Still, her friends protest. "No, no, I couldn't," or "I don't know how," or "I can't," or "It wouldn't turn out well." Yet Claire can tell by their questions that the women are drawn to the colors and canvases. Wanting to paint, yearning for color, wishing you could—these are the first stirrings of artistic leanings. "You really can," Claire encourages. "You just have to start."

Creativity is the ability that we all have to surpass ourselves. In midlife, we often feel as if we are less than we were before. We can't have babies, our bodies are changing, and our identities are in flux. Creativity allows us to go beyond our former limits, to tear down self-imposed barriers and realize even more of our potential. Regardless of our age, we want to express ourselves. "I don't need words or babies now," Claire says, "as much as I need paint and canvas."

> We can't have babies, our bodies are changing, and our identities are in flux. Creativity allows us to go beyond our former limits, to tear down self-imposed barriers and realize even more of our potential.

Creativity expands our repertoire. It loosens our grip on our inhibitions and allows us to play again, and at midlife that's a wonderful capacity to explore. "Color," says Claire, "is good for both the walls and my soul."

To Do or Not to Do

1. What creative expression interests you? Pay attention to what inspires you because that is creativity stirring.
2. Plant the playful seeds of intention by reading *The Little Engine That Could*.
3. Give yourself creative license. Set aside one morning each week to paint on something.
4. Make like a maverick. Hang out with folks who are expressing themselves in ways that interest you.
5. Imagine inviting friends over to view your finished canvas. When you are ready, call them up and set the date.

"Tell me, what is it you plan to do with
your one wild and precious life?"

—MARY OLIVER

Creative High

The week I wrote "Don't answer the phone" on the chalkboard above my desk, I was on a creative high. A creative high is experienced as electric, euphoric, absorbing, tingling, sparkling; it is a moment suspended in time. That week I was in a zone; time stood still. Something from the beyond was beckoning and I shut off the phone to be with it. Creative brilliance is something you can become receptive to, it's always there, but you have to reach down deep to tap in to it. Sometimes you have to retreat, shut the door, and be quiet. To get the creative high, you have to plug in to inspiration. To plug in to inspiration, you might need to close yourself off from all outside distractions. When we're involved in a creative project, we sometimes temporarily lose interest in socializing. It isn't that we're hermits or antisocial, because we're not trying to get away from people. Rather, our own inner fulfillment is leading us to shorter or longer periods of silence and creative pursuits. Isn't it odd that some people actually worry when this happens?

Have you seen the movie *Something's Gotta Give* with Diane Keaton? It's a movie with a heroine over forty-five, an actress over forty-five, and a writer-director (also a woman) over forty-five. It may be Hollywood, but that's a good omen. The movie honors middlescent women for their beauty and creativity. In the movie, the heroine, devastated after a love affair ends, isolates herself at her beach home and turns her heartache into a bestselling screenplay. She's cries and sobs—out loud. Not polite, Sunday-schoolgirl trickles, but open your lungs and let it out, belly-type sobs. She is not afraid of experiencing her pain and out of her fearlessness she lands in a creative zone. She goes through boxes and boxes of tissue. She wails alone and writes alone, no company, no distractions. She leans into her heartbreak and writes sentences, plots, characters, and an uplifting story. Solitude, plus hard work and dedication, seasoned with buckets of tears and laughter, add up to a creative high. She's out of her slump with renewed excitement. Sadness melts into satisfaction, heartache merges with a humorous spin, and presto— our heroine is even more fascinating than she was in the beginning.

That's the high that comes with honoring yourself and what you are going through. The creative spark is there and we find it more quickly when we pay attention to what is going on inside ourselves. Cry first if you feel like it, walk around the block if you are restless, then settle down and make friends with your story. By the time we have reached middle age, we all have suffered disappointments and broken hearts. When we are still, we may shed a few tears and in doing so we bring an added depth to whatever we are creating. A good cry gets the juices flowing. Don't you feel better after you have let yourself cry?

If you quiet down and go deep, you'll be less anxious, more centered, more charming. You might even come up with a few good sentences. You might come up with a play, poem, or short story. You might even stumble on a new art form.

We don't have to be sad to find that creative high, though. Malayna praises the benefits of retreating to do art. She was bleary-eyed from overworking and oversocializing. One night, when she was unable to sleep, she surfed the Net and serendipitously came upon an art form she wasn't familiar with—altered books.

An altered book is any book, old or new, that is used as a canvas and recycled by creative means into a work of art. They can be painted, cut, folded, collaged, gold-leafed, rubber stamped, or otherwise adorned. Malayna was instantly enamored. She had never considered herself creative, but something stirred within her, and she became a book rescuer and altered books. She said no to outside demands. She rescued books from garage sales and adorned them with images, poetry, clippings, beads, words, and handwritten letters. She revived her spirit by turning tattered books into art and memory books.

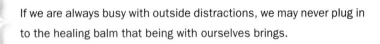

If we are always busy with outside distractions, we may never plug in to the healing balm that being with ourselves brings.

A creative high is joyous, grand, passionate, and miraculous. If we are always busy with outside distractions, we may never plug in to the healing balm that being with ourselves brings. When we run away from what is troubling us, we feel anxious and out of sorts, but when we sit with the ache and let ourselves simmer, something amazing comes forth. Isn't it wonderful to discover that we have so much range within ourselves?

To Do or Not to Do

1. Turn off the phone for a day and see what happens.
2. Leave a juicy message on your answering machine: "Can't talk now! I'm painting a masterpiece on the ceiling and writing my memoirs."
3. Wear a sign around your neck that says, "In silence." Simply nod and point to the sign when someone tries to talk to you.
4. Rescue books, adorn them, and turn them into art books.
5. Write letters in longhand. It is relaxing and more beautiful than e-mail. For encouragement, check out *www.letterexchange.com.*

"Creative spirits are truly ageless."

—SARK

Undomesticated Yearnings

Surya received the good news over the phone. "Congratulations! Your piece *The Proud One* has been selected to be part of the Bellevue Sculpture Exhibition." Surya was shocked by the acceptance. On opening night, twenty-four artists chosen from hundreds of entries from around the world were introduced to invited patrons and dignitaries. A jazz trio played in the background, guests nibbled on hors d'oeuvres, drank wine, and chatted. It was such a scene—artsy people, lively conversation, even the mayor was there. For Surya, it was a victory of major proportions, especially considering the childhood messages she has overcome.

Surya is fascinated with colors and shapes. As a child, she was intrigued with all varieties of art, from simple newspaper advertisements to delicate watercolors. She was especially enchanted by the watercolor peonies that her mother painted. "My mother painted some lovely peonies, but one day she said there was enough art already and she didn't want to contribute anymore." With that, her mother stopped painting and developed a hysterical streak. "Her anguish took over," says Surya.

From that point on, her mother devoted herself to her family and keeping the house clean. She dusted, vacuumed, baked, and did the laundry. She did everything for others and nothing for herself. She grew very despondent. Surya never fully understood why her mother stopped painting, but that decision influenced Surya's choices as well. "I had the same tendencies as my mother," says Surya, who put her own artistic dreams on the back burner when she got married. "My husband demanded all my attention," she says. She dabbled, doing a few drawings of her children when they were little, but nothing more.

Childhood messages are subtle and silent. They infuse our choices without us noticing, in ways we cannot describe. By midlife, we have all had the experience of catching ourselves behaving exactly like our mothers did and we are taken aback. It's a behavior that we swore we would never repeat, yet there we are, doing exactly what our mothers did. Surya wanted to paint, but she gave it up just like her mother had. It really doesn't matter what you call it—a midlife crisis, a wake-up call, or fate—but what matters is that after sixteen years in a stifling marriage, Surya took off her apron, hung up her broom, got divorced, and found her first job. They say that when we step out in the direction of our yearning unseen forces work on our behalf. That's what happened for Surya. The dreams that she had swept to the back started moving to the front of the line. It was serendipity and instant relief all at once, as the river of fate moved her along. Although she didn't have a formal art education, Surya got a job organizing art exhibitions and gallery shows. She was responsible for overseeing international artists invited to the city. She enjoyed it for sure, but in her heart she secretly yearned to be on the other side, to be one of the artists.

The years ticked on and exciting things happened. She hung out with artists, married again, and became a massage practitioner. She built a clientele, added an art studio in her home, and started painting sporadically. But then she was diagnosed with a cyst on her left eye. The doctor told her that it might eventually cause blindness, which caused Surya to change her outlook. "I suddenly realized that life is not forever. I had been thinking all along, 'I'll paint when I retire.' "

Since her diagnosis, Surya carries art supplies in her van and paints everywhere she goes, even on vacation. A large oil of herself and her mother hangs in the front hallway of her home. She painted the pink peonies that she grows in her garden and called them "My Mother's Peonies." She also takes classes and sculpts in addition to teaching a class titled "Painting Your Mother from Memory." "I'm active," she says. "That's the difference between being a dreamer of things you'll create and actually creating." She says, "Now I feel like I'm doing what I'm here for."

It took Surya twenty-two years to go from behind the scenes to the big time as an artist. Years ago, she wasn't creating anything and felt stifled in her life. Now her 5'9" sculpture, *The Proud One*, stands nobly next to the waterfall in the downtown park.

A midlife turning point can be a blessing if you heed it. It is a chance to sweep away the restrictions that we have imposed on ourselves from our youth—a wake-up call that life is not forever. It's a chance to step out in the direction of our dreams and let the unseen forces work on our behalf. So here's to Surya and midlife yearnings. Here's to taking our dreams off the back burner and creating whatever we choose. Now Surya cooks meals, cleans house, plants and weeds her garden, and gives massages, but she does not feel stifled or domesticated. She is an artist who is exploring herself, hanging out with other artists, and doing what she loves. She has gone beyond her childhood messages and is doing art.

To Do or Not to Do

1. Give up housework for a week and see what happens.
2. Be aware of childhood messages. Are there any stifling messages holding you back?
3. Carry art supplies in your car.
4. Buy an original piece of art.
5. Turn your home into a gallery and have your own art show.

*"Creative minds have always been known
to survive any kind of bad training."*

—ANNA FREUD

From Refrigerator to Rhinestones

Creative transitions don't often go in orderly sequences. Ellen learned this when life took her in a new direction. She got divorced at forty-seven and a year later she drove 1,000 miles round trip to drop off her twins at college. "I cried the entire 500 miles home," she remembers. "I felt like I'd left my kids and my identity in another state." For the first time in twenty-plus years, and in the middle of middlescence, Ellen was living on her own. Over the years, she'd fantasized about reading and sewing without interruption, but the first month in her empty house she was lethargic and disoriented. Each evening after work, instead of using her time as she had hoped, she lounged in front of the TV. Transitioning from meeting the needs of her family to meeting her own needs was difficult at first. Coworkers invited her to join them for drinks, but she usually declined. "I'd stop at the grocery store, buy food as if I were still shopping for a family, then go home and fill the refrigerator." Instead of cooking for herself, she'd throw together a salad, scramble an egg, or eat a bowl of cereal. "I was going through my days on automatic. I knew that I didn't need to stock the refrigerator, but I felt compelled."

Identities don't peel off easily. With no one to check in with or to cook for, Ellen was restless. "I'm good at caring for others," she says, "but I'm not as sharp when it comes to myself." For almost three decades, Ellen's role was wife and mother. It takes time and struggle to shake off those old routines. "I wanted to divorce my refrigerator and find other amusements for the dinner hour," she says, "but I keep repeating myself."

"I was sorting out, throwing away, and I sensed that I was redoing myself in the process."

One evening in a spurt of determination, Ellen drove past the market, went home, and instead of heading for the couch, she opened the refrigerator. She took everything out, wiped the shelves, and threw away the partially used relish, the unopened dressings, the outdated juice, the molding tomatoes, and the dried-out lettuce. In one hour, the refrigerator was gleaming and empty. The next week, she tackled the kitchen cupboards, and the following week she was up until 2 a.m. reorganizing the hall closets. "A bubonic cleaning bug took me over," she says. "I was sorting out, throwing away, and I sensed that I was redoing myself in the process." She sorted through her jewelry box and that was when she fell head over heels enchanted with seventeen antique rhinestone pins that her great-aunt had bequeathed her. As she looked at the beautiful vintage jewelry, she felt passion in her veins. "The sparkling crystals took my breath away," she says. She wore a different one to work each day—the dragonfly brooch, the flower-domed circle pin, the pink crystal butterfly clip. She adored them all. The jewels absorbed her, and she began searching for new, exciting ways to bring their beauty into her life.

Soon she'd forgotten all about cleaning and stocking the refrigerator and was spending the dinner hour focusing on her new love, researching the history of rhinestones at the library. That led to sewing satin and velveteen bags for safekeeping, which led to browsing antique stores for new treasures. The last time I spoke with Ellen, she was taking her third jewelry class and restoring and producing original designs.

That's how passion is. It arises out of a combination of taking it easy, cleaning out or getting rid of what doesn't fit, and reforming yourself. It's in the midst of clearing out our physical and emotional space that our creative urges are heard. When we follow them, they take over us, consume us, and lead us someplace that we hadn't considered going before.

To Do or Not to Do

1. Give yourself time to make all midlife transitions. When you drop the kids off at college, give yourself time to adjust.
2. Take it easy on the couch for as long as you need to. That's perfectly acceptable.
3. Take note of where your identity is stuck. Stocking the refrigerator when you're the only one living in the house is a sign that you might need to move on.
4. Welcome the bubonic cleaning bug. While cleaning out closets, drawers, and refrigerators, you're clearing corners of your psyche in the process.
5. Revamp yourself with rhinestones. Every lady needs sparkle.

"Don't agonize. Organize."

—Florynce Kennedy

Genius Emerging . . .

1. You'd rather do it yourself than hire a decorator.
2. You read cookbooks for fun, clip recipes, and have piles of them to organize.
3. You collect scraps of paper with your favorite sentences to use in the book that you intend to write someday.
4. Your house and garden are becoming more important than gossip, news, or being right.
5. You buy art books from the bargain table, you attend art openings, and you are surprisingly attracted to paint brushes.
6. You're signing up for lessons.
7. You adore the domestic arts—rearranging the furniture, cooking, sewing, gardening, entertaining.

Artiste de Ma Vie

Children are naturally creative. Give a child a box of crayons, markers, and a stack of paper, and soon they're scribbling colorful lines and painting rainbows. Five-year-old Carly draws yellow-orange suns that take up a whole sheet of paper. She's also good at daisy chains; people with long, spider legs; pink frogs; green cats; and blue trees with red apples. She's absorbed by her artwork and when she's finished, she unselfconsciously gives it all away. Carly's mom hangs the masterpieces on the refrigerator or frames them to give to the grandparents. Carly's creations make everyone happy. Creativity is like that; it accentuates the playful and brings out the joy. Do you remember that satisfaction?

Sadly, our creativity gets squelched and takes a back seat to all our obligations as we grow older. At school, it's "don't color outside the lines," then it's, "put the crayons away." The focus turns to memorizing facts, history, science, reading, and arithmetic. It's rules, rules, rules. Rules for thinking and rules for behaving. With so many rules about how to be a human being, the creative spark gets brushed aside, pushed down, and squished. With so many rules, by the time we reach adolescence, we start believing and acting as if there's only one right way to do and only one right way to be. It's as if there is only one way to think, one way to draw, one way to live. After all that creativity bashing, the creative fire has been reduced to a flicker.

When we think of our lives as our own creations, happily we discover that at midlife the authentic spark still shines.

Then it's higher education and the goal of moneymaking. You're constantly told, "You can't make money being an artist," and so once again you squelch that longing and focus on sensible, lucrative actions. You build a career, find a partner, have children, and make a home. As you settle down, your creative inclinations bubble up. Your one-of-a-kind style pushes forth and, fortunately, it has a way of seeping into every day. There it is, reflected in the pillows you choose for the couch, the color you paint the kitchen walls, the style of the bedspread, the books you buy, the names that you give your children. Still, you don't think of yourself as creative or artistic. Old conditioning sticks.

Perhaps you have the mistaken notion that being creative or artistic is only for the few accomplished folks. Perhaps you bought into the notion that only a few select individuals in this world are creative. Perhaps you've been focusing on others so long that you've lost sight of your own potential. Modern-day brain research confirms that our capacity for creativity is much greater than we could ever imagine! Each of us is gifted with a birthright of unlimited possibility. Each of us is packaged in a one-of-a-kind wrapping made up of our talents and dreams. No two people on this planet are alike, and because of that fact alone we're all destined to be artists. When we think of our lives as our own creations, happily we discover that at midlife the authentic spark still shines. At middlescence, we can once again embrace that child who likes to paint rainbows.

To Do or Not to Do

1. Buy the biggest box of crayons and the biggest piece of paper, and make big yellow shining suns. Then display them on your refrigerator or give them away.
2. Drape a scarf around your neck, Parisian-style. Accentuate with color.
3. Pretend, imagine, and change your old routine.
4. Take artistic inventory of your home. What signs of individuality do you see?
5. Choose one room and rearrange it according to your whims.
6. Christen yourself "Artiste de Ma Vie."

"There is vitality, a life force, an energy, a quickening that is translated through you into action, and because there is only one of you in all of time, this expression is unique. And if you block it, it will never exist through any other medium and be lost."

—Martha Graham

Inspired Ingredients

Gigi spent years as a sous chef, hired to cook what others instructed her to. She earned experience and confidence on the job, but since she hit forty or so, she's been expanding her expertise. Gigi's an inspired cook. Everyone loves to gather in her kitchen and sample her concoctions. Fresh ingredients and nuts excite her. She calls them "inspired ingredients." What are inspired ingredients? They are the ingredients that you might not expect, the ones she adds on a whim, the ones that she hadn't planned on using but did. They add surprise. With a sprinkle of this and handful of that, she'll turn a mundane, middle-of-the-week dinner into gastronomical pleasure. Take hazelnuts, for example. Gigi adds hazelnuts to the most ordinary ingredients. She mixes hazelnuts with gorgonzola cheese and adds that to hamburger. Voila! When grilled and topped with zucchini, those plain burgers turn into the gourmet-est burgers around. She puts hazelnuts in spicy orange sauce and pours it over chicken. She mixes hazelnuts with apricot jam and bakes the concoction into scones. Hazelnuts and marshmallow sauce, warmed and dripped over berries and bananas, are decadently delightful. Nuts of all kinds, cilantro, fresh limes, lemons, and vanilla are staples in her pantry.

What is inspiration? And once a woman is inspired, what makes her follow through? For Gigi, it's exuberance about cooking and trying new combinations. While some artists are inspired to sculpt or paint on canvas, Gigi's inspiration is of the culinary kind. Just as a painter is inspired by an idea and puts brush to canvas, Gigi waits for such inspirations to drop into her kitchen. She once plucked the idea "put lemons on pizza" from the sky and immediately followed the direction without hesitation. Born out of this inspiration was the one and the only chicken pizza topped with lemon, cilantro, and pistachios. Gigi throws caution to the wind and goes for it. She takes risks. She's playful and unconcerned with rules.

No matter what our medium of expression, we all can be inspired. By the time we have reached middlescence, we know the rules well enough to know which ones to amend. We are energized by our creative ventures. We are getting over our tendency to hold ourselves back and play it safe. We have to believe that it's OK to put lemons on pizza, limes on corn, or chocolate on peanut butter toast. We have made it to our forties and that, combined with our experience and inspired manifestations, makes for satisfied living.

The way Gigi cooks is a wonderful inspiration for all of us, in more than one way. Instead of following the recipes exactly, both in the kitchen and in life, at middlescence we have earned the right to deviate. The next time you're inspired, go with it! Do something unexpected instead of looking for step-by-step instructions.

No matter what our medium of expression, we all can be inspired. We have to believe that it's OK to put lemons on pizza.

Gigi's going beyond her training and creating new experiences for herself. She's using her instincts to take her in new directions. Knowledge without inspiration turns flat and boring, but inspiration combined with experience makes it possible to dream up something new. Inspiration says we can triumph over adversity. We can turn the bitter into beneficial. We can put lemons on pizza. We can put hazelnuts in hamburgers. We can cook, eat, and live by our inspirations.

To Do or Not to Do
1. Pay attention to your inspirations. Keep track of them, write them down, and see where they take you. Collect inspirational quotes and let them inspire you.

2. Add one unexpected ingredient to whatever you're cooking for dinner.

3. Get comfortable with nuts. Buy nuts, cook with nuts, and hang out with nuts (also known as artists).

4. Design an inspiration pantry and fill it with inspired ingredients.

5. Combine your experience with your inspiration and see what concoctions you come up with.

―――

"I had no idea what I wanted to do with my life until I was thirty-seven years old. I'm very lucky that I finally found out."

—JULIA CHILD

Get Out of Bed

I sleep like a baby—in spurts. In my twenties I could sleep for twelve hours straight. In my thirties I slept whenever my baby slept. In my forties I was up late at night waiting for my teenager to come home. Now I sleep four hours here, three hours there. I used to worry about not sleeping in eight hour stretches. That was before I discovered that many creative geniuses are up all night fooling around with predawn inspirations. Tossing and turning is not for me. If I wake up, I get up. If I'm tired, I take a nap. Years ago when I was caught up in striving to make something of myself, I pushed my body to sleep eight hours in a row. I thought I needed continuous shut-eye to function. I don't. Now that I'm more interested in my inner world, now that I'm not on a 9–5 schedule, I prefer to follow my body's rhythm and see where it takes me.

There's so much in the dark, if you take the time to embrace it.

There's so much in the dark, if you take the time to embrace it. Darkness is not dependent on time. There's no hustle, no scramble, no exertion. Even the most mundane activities, like ironing, are timeless. You don't have to get it done or wear it because you don't have any appointments to rush off to. There are no phone calls or schedules. No one is watching over your shoulder to make sure you complete your tasks. It's liberating to get out of bed and roam the house in the middle of the night. You can be selfish and strange and uninhibited and no one scolds you. In the middle of the night, there's much to be revealed.

Creativity, like a seed, springs up from darkness. Inspiration arises from that blessed silence underneath. Darkness is essential for all life to begin. Senna, an artist, has always had trouble with insomnia. For years, she worried about not being able to get to sleep, and she relied on sleeping pills. "After my last bout of insomnia," Senna told me, "it dawned on me that without darkness there is no flash of light." After that light bulb of understanding, she lost her fear of not sleeping, threw away her sleeping pills, and paints instead of worrying.

Why do we force ourselves to stay in bed when we can't sleep? I've done a lot of thinking, and I'm sure it's because people worry about doing something in the darkness that doesn't conform to what they do in the light of day—they're afraid of doing something out of character. I'm sympathetic to this because I used to be the same way. But now I embrace it. I have fun with it. I am slightly extravagant at night and prone to all kinds of nonsense—and I'm loving every minute of it. During one of my midnight whims, I converted my basement into the Institute of Art and Letters. I began the project at 3 A.M. by painting the walls pink. From there, I didn't stop. For a week, my frenzy continued until the stairs were cherry red and the floor turquoise accentuated with silvery shapes. My body was sore, that's true, and I fell asleep soaking in Epson salts, but I chalk it up to making friends with the night. Call me crazy, but it is my space, my glory, and my precious time that makes these wonderful happenings possible.

I have big dreams for the Institute. I imagine inviting other creative types—artists, writers, philosophers, dancers, Meryl Streep, Sister Wendy, and the mystics—to come over, give classes, hold salons, iron, eat dark chocolate, and watch the sun come up. So the next time you can't sleep, get out of bed! Make friends with the darkness and see where it takes you. You may just find that you shine more brightly in the middle of the night than you do during the day!

To Do or Not to Do

1. Experiment with darkness. If you can't sleep, get up and roam around the house.
2. Eat one expensive dark chocolate truffle. Dark chocolate is the very best tranquilizer, much better than a sleeping pill.
3. Sleep in spurts. Babies do, so why can't you?
4. Make friends with the night. Sleep in tune with your creative cycle. Throw away your sleeping pills and do something out of character.
5. Open an institute in your basement. Invite me over to teach a class and we'll watch the sun rise together.

"Creativity—like human life—begins in darkness."

—JULIA CAMERON

What Makes You Come Alive?

What are your longings? What makes you come alive?

It's never too late to be beautiful, exuberant, and slightly sassy, and it's never to late to wash a car, wear a strapless bra, or dance the Argentine tango.

According to Lee, the Argentine tango is a really cool dance. One French guy she was dancing with said that when a couple dances the Argentine tango they look like they're in love, and when the very same couple dances the American tango they look like they're about to get a divorce! I don't know if everyone would see it that way, but according to Lee, the Argentine tango is wild, free, and sexy—but it's also extremely orchestrated. "Getting really good at it is like getting a doctorate in chemistry because there's so much to learn and it takes plenty of practice," Lee says. But Lee is going for it. "The men in my classes are cool, intellectual, educated, and mostly financially solvent." All side benefits for taking up tango, don't you agree? "They're not hitting on you for immediate sex," she says. "They're sincerely interested in the tantric experience of tango dancing as an exquisite end in itself." Now if that description isn't enough to urge us all to sign up, then we're either extremely tired or already completely satisfied. "Women of all ages are valued for their ability to tune in and follow skillfully," Lee says, "and perhaps somewhat for dressing 'tangoistically,' but not so much for how they look." For those of us who really like to dance, but are getting too old and too exhausted with being hit on, this seems to be an elegant solution.

It's never too late to wash a car, wear a strapless bra, or dance the Argentine tango.

Tango is passionate melodies, wrenchingly wild rhythms, and lush movements. It's about the passion of longing. We can all relate to that. We have all felt that sweet heartache and yearned for passionate connections. Longings lead us from the material to the nonmaterial, from the physical to the nonphysical, from our senses to the spiritual. In the second half of life, our desires fade from searching for that which is outside ourselves to that which is within, for something deeper. We search for our essence.

Ask yourself: What makes me come alive? Do that more often.

My mother is still discovering all kinds of things about herself, from the practical to the spiritual. She washed her car for the first time when she was eighty-two years old. Dad washed all the cars once a week, and after he died, Mom took her car to the car wash for the first time. She had to learn how to fill up with gas, too. She mastered it, but she doesn't necessarily like doing it. I'm sure she longs for Dad and wishes he were here. She doesn't remember what prompted her to wash her car, but she discovered that she could do it by herself if she has to.

That same summer, Mom got her first strapless bra. My sister Kathy took her shopping to buy a dress for a granddaughter's wedding. You should see Mom in that dress. A long black skirt with a white strapless top and a silvery white jacket that matches her hair perfectly. She makes a statement in that dress; she's the grand dame of the ball. When I see Mom looking so radiant, I long for Dad, too. He would be beaming. We tell her how beautiful she is, but I'm sure it doesn't fill up that space that she keeps for Dad. Even though she misses Dad, she says that with each new adventure, she is pleased with herself. She is speaking up in a way she had never done when Dad was around. When she took a history class at the college last summer, she told the instructor, "I didn't take this class to participate orally." At her age she can take college classes and participate, or not, if she chooses. Mom likes to go places, but since she no longer drives on freeways, she hired a driver to take her to town.

What space are you keeping inside yourself? What are your secret desires? Andrea's secret desire is to sing in a Broadway-type musical production. Perhaps in a little theater somewhere. "Playing some small part in the play, wearing an old-fashioned dress, singing the songs, and being part of the love story really excite me," she says. "So far I haven't had the courage to even audition for a chorus role, but maybe someday."

"I always envisioned myself singing," Aletha says. "I have a good voice, but it's untrained." She has the time and money now, so she's taking private lessons with an instructor at the university. "I want to sing onstage with Willie Nelson. I have a fantasy that we'll wear matching red headbands." Willie isn't getting any younger, so she has to hurry.

We all have longings. Why not follow and see where they lead? Lee is taking her first vacation in twenty years and flying to Buenos Aires for tango classes. She still can't even believe she's going, but "I'm slashing and resewing clothes like mad in preparation." Aletha is now singing. "I had my first lesson," she wrote. "The instructor wants me to sing Italian love songs, but I opted for show tunes."

The world needs more women who have come alive. Ask yourself what makes you come alive and do that more often.

To Do or Not to Do

1. Ask yourself: What makes me come alive? Do that more often.

2. Do you have any secret longings? Is there something you would like to try, but haven't? If you are over forty, go for it now.

3. Act as if . . . Act as if you already are a great dancer, singer, or poet.

4. Say what you feel, especially if you feel like saying it. Otherwise, be quiet.

5. Sign up for tango lessons or singing lessons, audition for a musical, wash your car, and wear a strapless bra.

"The journey in between what you once were and who you are now becoming is where the dance of life really takes place."

—BARBARA DE ANGELIS

Marvelous Butcher Paper Art

1. Buy six feet of colored butcher paper and draw big, big flowers. Cut them out and hang them on the wall. When you tire of them, use them as wrapping paper.

2. Buy five feet of white butcher paper. Use watercolors to paint a soft background. When the paint is dry, fill up the paper with inspirational quotes. Use it as a one-of-a-kind disposable wall hanging and/or wrapping paper.

3. Buy four feet of butcher paper and a mailing tube. With colored marking pens, write a handwritten letter to a friend. Mail it in the tube. Wait by the phone for her response.

4. Buy three feet of butcher paper. Trace your hand and the hands of your beloved ones. Write loving descriptive words around each hand.

5. Buy two feet of butcher paper. Go to a coffee shop. Using black marking pens, write down all your regrets. Take it home and burn it in the fireplace.

6. Buy one foot of butcher paper and fill it up with doodles.

Section Five . . .

Mourning Glory and

SACRED SPACES

When we get to be a certain age—the exact age is different for everyone—we begin to think a whole lot about aging. We begin thinking about dying, crumbling, and fading away. Growing gracefully is to bend and go without resistance. It's allowing ourselves to be taken. The more graceful we are, the better we look. Resistance to bending is what looks bad, not wrinkles.

Papier-Mâché Artist

If it wasn't love at first sight, it was, at the very least, infatuation. When I stepped into the housewares boutique and saw the voluptuous, brightly colored bowl in the middle of the table next to the back wall, I walked straight toward her, ignoring the linen napkins that I'd gone into the store for in the first place.

The bowl was papier-mâché, crafted in seductive colors of pink, purple, and sunny yellow flowers swirling in a field of soft green grass. She took my breath away. I was smitten, faint with excitement, and giddy. I lifted her up. She was one of a kind, a real beauty and light as a feather. I imagined her sitting regally on my white kitchen counter. She was a star that truly commanded the limelight. I fell head over heels and I wanted to take her home.

"Isn't she gorgeous?" the clerk said. "An original by an artist from Mexico. We had six, she's the last one."

"How much for her?" I asked the clerk.

"Five hundred ninety-seven dollars."

My heart sank. She was out of my league. I said my goodbyes, sat her down gently, and walked away.

My sweetheart, William, who was being very patient considering that he hadn't been feeling well, offered to buy it for me. I couldn't let him, plus he was tired and ready to go home. "I wonder how she was made?" I said out loud on the way home in the car—I couldn't stop talking about her. "I wish I could make a bowl like that. Maybe I can learn papier-mâché."

"I bet you can," William encouraged.

Two days later I sat by William's side at the doctor's office when he got the diagnosis. We hadn't expected it—we thought he had caught a virus on his last trip to India. "You have non-Hodgkin's lymphoma," the doctor said. "If you have to have cancer, this is the best kind to have," the nurse confided to us when the doctor left the room. A few minutes later, the doctor reversed that prognosis and told us that William's cancer was the most aggressive form.

William's tumor grew with lightning speed. His arms shriveled and his chest atrophied while his belly grew to gigantic proportions. He was badly winded—just getting up a flight of stairs took tremendous effort. Taking a full breath was a virtual impossibility.

"I'd like to buy you that papier-mâché bowl," he told me one morning six months later. "That's so sweet," I said, "but I don't want you to spend that much money right now." Another time, William announced, "Dying is creative."

"What do you mean?"

"In the process of creating, something not of this world starts happening within you and you start to disappear. That's the same with dying," he said. "I'm starting to disappear." Then he surprised me with a coffee table book on papier-mâché. The inscription read: "To my sweet papier-mâché artist. In the hope that this will not be our last year together." I cried and learned a lot that year about death and loving, grief and papier-mâché.

When William was told that the tumor was not responding to treatment, we realized, of course, that he might soon die, that the day of his departure from this world was not off somewhere in a vague future but that it was imminent, that the chapters of our life together had all been written and the book was more or less complete and ready for the bookbinder. Though it struck me as ludicrous that our life might be over and about to terminate without some sort of grand finale, some breakthrough or significant accomplishment, some fanfare, I had to face the fact that this indeed might be "it."

Creativity comforts me—it's like a little promise reminding me that death did not destroy the love that was and is between us.

William surrendered to chemo and radiation and I surrendered to paper and paste. The last three months of William's life we both knew death was coming, and with death so near, we stopped making plans. That's what happens. Tomorrow disappears. All the dramas that were being played out on TV—both the soap operas and the news—William would never know what happened to any of them because he wouldn't be here anymore. William said that he was sorry that we couldn't make our trip to Bali. I told him it didn't matter because we were as close as we had ever been. It didn't matter because we didn't need to get away to enjoy each other, we no longer needed entertainment to have fun. We didn't need anything but each other.

There wasn't much to talk about, so we held hands. I tore paper strips and he watched as I learned to make papier-mâché. That's the blessing that comes from living with death so near—distractions disappear. We laughed, cried, and reviewed our ten years together. We fell in love again. William left his body peacefully and I was at his side. I've made ten bowls and more than 100 bracelets since then. Creativity comforts me—it's like a little promise reminding me that death did not destroy the love that was and is between us.

To Do or Not to Do

1. When faced with loss, do a little something for the artist within you. Creativity plugs us into the universal truth that love never disappears.
2. Give papier-mâché a whirl. For inspiration, look at the beautiful book that William gave me, *The Art and Craft of Papier-Mâché* by Juliet Bawden (Chronicle, 1995).
3. View creativity as a meditation. Focus on allowing something from beyond to take over you.
4. Pour love into those you love.
5. Love well so that when death comes you will have no regrets.

"Whenever creativity calls you, go with it. It is God calling you."

—OSHO

Wake-up Calls

We all get at least one or two wake-up calls. A beloved one dies and we are reminded how short life is. A spouse drinks too much, we lose a job, or the things we planned don't go in an orderly manner. We get a lump in our breast and it's cancer, we have a financial setback, we get divorced. For some of us the wake-up calls are subtler. Our bodies ache in ways we hadn't expected. There are bumps in our plans that take us in another direction. We get stopped in our tracks. We hanker for something more.

Wake-up calls are spiritual stirrings. They remind us that we are not only physical beings, but spiritual beings as well. Wake-up calls help us pay closer attention to the longings of our souls. Wake-up calls beseech us to review our lives, to slow down, to honor our inner wisdom, to take a closer look and reevaluate. We know that running over our intuition, our inner voice, avoiding its direction, and pushing our unconscious messages under will get us into more trouble. And so we are forced to slow down in order for our authentic selves to emerge.

From dull pain to major crises, from a personal inventory to a spiritual quest, these are the themes of life's second half. We realize that half of our life is over. Perhaps we skipped over what matters most and we do not want to do that any longer. We want to soak up all the joy. We want to grow spiritually. We ask questions: What is meaningful? What brings us joy? Where do we want to put our attention? What is our intention?

Marian had several wake-up calls that left her trembling. Within six months, her father died, her dog died, and she was in a car wreck that left her with a permanent limp. That was enough to send her into a state of grief that lasted for a couple of years. "Life is too short," she finally said, and she changed her ways. She gave up smoking. She stopped drinking. She moved out of the fast lane and on to easy street. Now she studies tai chi. She took her sailboat out of storage and uses it. She hosts potluck suppers and entertains friends.

Wake-up calls push us and shake us into becoming all that we are meant to be.

As painful as wake-up calls might be, they are a necessity. They are built into the psyche. Without such a summons, we might remain permanently shallow. Wake-up calls remind us that if we are to become our authentic selves, we must start now. They push us and shake us into becoming all that we are meant to be. The transformation that comes when we take care of the needs of our souls is remarkable. We become more than we ever imagined. We become softer, wiser, and fulfilled. Our lives become wider, deeper, and happier. We become lighter. Wake-up calls demand that we express ourselves in ways that lift our spirits higher and help us soar.

To Do or Not to Do

1. Ask yourself, Have you had a wake-up call? How did you answer?
2. Move from the fast lane to easy street.
3. Sow the seeds of happiness by inviting friends over for potlucks.
4. Find time. Take up tai chi. Learn to sail. Find time for yourself.
5. Stop smoking. Drink minimally. Eat green.

"There is a universal sense in all of us of having lost something precious in life, and of trying to return to the place where we hope it exists."

—BRENDA SHOSHANNA, PH.D.

Little Love Objects

Ellen fell into a slump when her youngest child, Riley, turned sixteen and got a driver's license. Ellen had been a mother driving kids around for twenty-six years, and now her car and her nest, while not completely empty, were vacant most of the time. Riley had wheels, friends, a part-time job, a boyfriend, and volleyball. She managed her own social life, homework, and cell phone. Like all active teenagers, Riley didn't have much patience for her mother's questions: How was school today? Where are you going? Did you get your homework done? Do you want to go shopping? Be home by eleven? When barraged with that line of motherly cross-examination, Riley balked. "Mom, I'm busy!" or "Leave me alone!" she'd snap before closing the door to her bedroom. When Riley did come around, the two of them squabbled. They had those mother-daughter quarrels about the inconsequential towels on the floor and the messy bedroom. They had six months' worth of quarrels about nothing, but underneath the surface a shift in their relationship was brewing. As Riley became more independent, Ellen's motherly duties were becoming obsolete. The quarrels about curfews and allowance were really quarrels about separating. They were cutting the cord and disguising the pain of separation as teenage insubordination.

When you've been watching over children, when they have been the center of your world, and when the whirlwind of excitement doesn't always include you, you feel left out. "I've been discarded," Ellen said. "She doesn't need me any more." Ellen had known that her role would evaporate someday, she just hadn't expected the ending to be so abrupt. She had thought that Riley would be her companion at least for a few more years. The older kids were out of state, the house was quiet, and Ellen was lonely. She was disoriented. Riley had been the object of her affections, her buddy, her sidekick, and her sweet shopping chum. "Mom, I know what it's like to be with you, now I want to be with my friends." Ellen hoped to do fun things with her daughter. "Would you like to go to Vancouver for the weekend?" "Mom, I can't be away from my friends all weekend!"

Ellen was shocked, sad, and a little mad. "It's not fair," she said. She was restless, agitated, and in a crummy mood. "What will I do if I'm not a mother?" Ellen asked. What will she do with no one to depend upon her? Where will she shower her love?

To go from overseeing children to overseeing yourself is challenging and a little heartbreaking.

Letting go of active-duty mothering is difficult. To go from overseeing children to overseeing yourself is challenging and a little heartbreaking. It demands some deep soul searching. When your identity is tied closely with your children, when your focus has been making sure they are fed, clothed, and well cared for. When you have been saying "Wear your coat," "Go to bed," and "Dinner is ready" for twenty years, it takes concentration and a little creative action to stop. When you have been absorbed cheering them on, it's painful to shift the focus off them and on to yourself. Your darling children have been the center of your world, they have been in the spotlight, and you took very good care of them. They were your little love objects. You liked it that way. Sometimes watching your love objects grow up feels like one gigantic loss. Unless of course you discover a new passion. Unless you discover other objects for your affections.

Ellen is a lady who handles pain by piling on projects. When she gets anxious, she makes sure she's busy so that she doesn't have to think.

Usually she busies herself with cleaning projects—and there are always plenty of them. When she cleans, you know she's upset. For one year, she cleaned closets and reorganized. She had a super-duper garage sale. She cleaned the garage and reorganized the family photos. She baked cookies and sent the older kids care packages. During it all, she had a sinking feeling that she couldn't explain. What she didn't realize was that as she cleaned out the house, her psyche was rearranging itself. What was her purpose? she wondered. She sat on the couch and stared. She fell into a slump. What's a mother who liked being a mother to do?

She joined a book club and read. She put in long hours at her job, came home, and roamed around the house. She exercised. It wasn't enough. She volunteered two hours a month, and while it was satisfying to do good deeds, that didn't completely fuel the fire in her heart. Her identity was shaken and her future seemed bleak. Who was she if she wasn't a mother?

We place an enormous unconscious burden on our families and children to meet all our needs. When our nest is almost empty, it throws us for a loop. Our children cannot fill us up completely and we do not expect them to, but it takes some soul searching to discover where to place all our passion.

That's what some women call a midlife crisis—a crack in the lens of how we view ourselves. A midlife crisis is a break in our infrastructure and that results in lots of upheavals. Our role as a mom is unsteady, our mother identity is melting. There is a tear in our security blanket. Who to love? Who will love us? How to express love to those little ones who are all grown up? This is the essence of a mother's midlife crisis.

That's what some women call a midlife crisis—a crack in the lens of how we view ourselves.

We all need little love objects. Little containers to express our goodwill, compassion, and kindness. Ellen is a thoughtful, creative, sentimental, expressive woman who sends cards for all occasions. That's how she discovered stamping. One day she wanted to send a note to a friend but she didn't have any cards around, so she made one. She cut out a picture of her friend, pasted it on card stock, sewed ribbon around the edges, and wrote a four-line poem. And voilà! She'd made a charming card that said more than one she could have purchased. Well, you know how one thing leads to another. Within a few months, Ellen had discovered the art of stamping and was taking classes. Designing and creating cards has become her passion. She pours good wishes into her cards and sends them to the people she cares about. The act of creating keeps her connected. She is also thinking about getting a puppy. She wants wiggly companions. She wants to cuddle little beings.

In addition to our family members, we all need circles of love beyond them. We need community, comforting friends, and sassy fellow travelers. We all need warmth. We need love objects to shower our affections into and onto. We need to receive love as well. We need to wrap up in love and get cozy. Our hearts and souls are made for loving. It is in loving that we find deep security, safety, and satisfaction. It is in the loving of another that we are most grounded. Love objects are the antidotes to feeling abandoned.

To Do or Not to Do

1. Hold on. When your kids become teens, you will start acting a little teenagery yourself.
2. Do not badger your teens. Only three questions per day allowed.
3. Ask yourself the questions that you've been asking them.

4. Adopt love objects. Become a love object yourself. Let others mother you for a change.

5. Pour all that motherly love into something wiggly, girly, soft, sweet, and tender.

―――――

"Sometime in your life you will go on a journey. It will be the longest journey you have ever taken. It is the journey to find yourself."

—KATHERINE SHARP

A Studio of Her Own

Menopause has its blessing because it releases us empty-nesters from the question that crosses all of our minds from time to time: Should I have another baby? We might be wistful about abandoned childhood bedrooms and the nurseries of long ago. We might ask ourselves, What else is there for me to do? But if this book has taught you one thing, it's that there's plenty to do! And what do empty-nesters do when the kids are grown and out of the house? They turn bedrooms into studios.

What matters is that we have a private space to be alone and quiet. A place to go, to close the door, to drop out, and to tune in.

Every woman needs a studio, no matter what her passion— sewing, painting, quilting, knitting, sculpting, writing. Size is not important. The studio can be the size of a closet—it may actually be a closet that we've cleared out. What matters is that we have a private space to be alone and quiet. A place to go, to close the door, to drop out, and to tune in. A place to listen and put our visions down. A studio is like a playhouse—only for adults. As girls we played in sandboxes and climbed tree houses. We served tea to dolls and teddy bears in doll-houses. We put on puppet shows in backyard tents, built cardboard forts, and met in secret clubhouses. At middlescence we're wildly creative once again and ready for a grown-up hideaway.

Simone is remodeling her home. Walls are coming down and the entire space is being opened up. "I've always wanted to live in a loft, but I can't afford one so I'm redoing my rambler to look like one." Her neighbors shake their heads and think she's silly. A realtor friend advised that tearing down walls is bad for resale. Simone is bravely following her instincts and not acquiescing to outside suggestions; she's following her gut. "I want my entire house to be my studio," she says. She's letting loose and trying out ideas. She's adding freestanding beams to hold up the ceiling. "I want wild motif and open space."

Kelly's studio is in the garage. She goes there every day before and after her part-time job. She throws pots on the wheel, fires them in the kiln, and paints the bowls and vases at the long, paint-stained table. "Art is more than what I produce," she says, "it's a way of living." Some days Kelly doesn't produce a thing, she just stands around and soaks up the vibe. She's in love with her studio, she gets high being there, and she goes mad with the wonder of it all. She painted the cement floor bright purple and lime green.

When my daughter, Amanda, moved out I created my own studio—I turned the basement into the Institute of Art and Letters. The stairs to the Institute are Opi Red to match the walls upstairs, the floor turquoise and silver, the walls bright pink. It's a cheerful space for dabbling. I turned her bedroom into my writing studio. I put the computer next to the window so I can look out at the lake when I'm writing. It is thrilling to be at this stage of my life. I can turn the whole house into a creative space. I intend to hold classes there and invite artists, writers, and midlifers to come over and teach. I like linking up artist to artist, because the energy is really outrageous then.

You can go wild decorating a studio. A studio is an imagination factory and so let your instincts lead. This is not the space for holding back and conforming. The studio is where we fall in love again, where we expand our hearts, open up our souls, and express ourselves. The studio is a divine space for divine work in divine time. We've gotta have it, it's in our blood.

To Do or Not to Do

1. Clean out a room or a closet and make it your studio. Take a look at the book *The House to Ourselves: Reinventing Home Once the Kids Are Grown* by Todd Lawson and Tom Connor (Taunton Press, 2004).
2. Decorate your studio in wild motif. When people ask you what you are doing with your soon-to-be-empty nest, you can tell them you're turning it into a studio.
3. Link up with artists and visit their studios.
4. Give praise to the universe, the sky, and the earth, the source of all creativity.
5. Go to your studio daily. Hang out, roll around, and soak up the vibe.

"Art is not about thinking something up.
It is about the opposite—getting something down."

—Julia Cameron

Emotional Bravery

Women in their forties, fifties, and sixties are no longer doomed to suffering in bad marriages. In fact, according to AARP research, two-thirds of divorces after age forty are initiated by wives, debunking the myth of an older man divorcing his wife for a younger woman.

At age forty-two, Renee left her husband and the security of her corporate position to follow her dream of going to the Art Institute. She was gutsy, and resigned from her job before her divorce was even settled. That's the way it is these days.

"There were too many problems," says Renee, "and my husband was oblivious to them. I wanted out of my marriage and I wanted to finish my degree in design." Risking it all requires that we sometimes have to leap without thinking about all the consequences. When we really want something, sometimes we have to put our rational objections aside and jump before we lose our nerve. And even though there were some tough times ahead, that's just what Renee did.

Following the beat of your own drummer can be a bumpy ride. "Sometimes I think I should have left my marriage sooner and sometimes I think I should have kept my job longer." It happens to all of us. We make decisions and things turn out badly, but then when it's over we can look back and call it experience.

Following the beat of your own drummer can be a bumpy ride. We make decisions and things turn out badly, but then when it's over we can look back and call it experience.

Well, Renee had a smorgasbord of experiences, bad luck, poor judgment, and heartbreaks before she figured it out and got to that peaceful other side. The house didn't sell quickly enough, so she couldn't count on her share of the profit to pay for tuition or books. She maxed out a credit card trying to deal with expenses, and her mother called multiple times each day with a request, a complaint, or a catastrophe. Pansy, her cat, had surgery and the astronomical vet bill went on her other credit card. "My disasters came in threes. Three, three, and when I thought I was in the clear there were three more upsets."

In the middle of her second semester at school, Renee's Pap smear came back and the doctor recommended a hysterectomy, which resulted in oophorectomy, the removal of her ovaries, and abruptly threw her into menopause. Some women may glide through menopause with few, if any, problems but Renee's symptoms were exaggerated; she had them all—hot flashes, aching joints, mood swings, and absolutely no energy except for bouncing off the walls. In the midst of midterm exams she was a bundle of rage and sorrow.

With so many upheavals, it was hard for Renee to figure how much of her torment was a result of hormones and how much was a psychological reaction to all the change and loss she was going through. One day during this time, she snapped in front of her classmates. "I know I have so much to look forward to," she said, "but I feel like my life is ending." Renee's biggest fear was that she was losing control of her emotions and turning into a "hysterical, dried-up old shrew."

Throughout all of this, Renee felt irritable, cranky, tearful, impatient, anxious, insecure, and full of self-doubt. But that was not all that she was. She was also funny, energetic, spunky, creative, and brave. She was hard on herself, but she demonstrated time and time again that she was emotionally brave. She was pleasant and kind to her mother, she was honest and firm with her soon-to-be ex, she apologized quickly when she snapped at her friends, she cried and took long walks when she was lonely or mad, and she took care of her body. She got acupuncture and massages, took naps in the middle of the day. She wrote and drew in a journal. She studied and got good grades. She was doing all these things, but wasn't giving herself any credit. She had so much emotional bravery, but she didn't see it.

When the school year ended, the anxiety and irritability ended too, and Renee discovered that she hadn't turned into a prune. She had faced her fears, and her zest for living was renewed. She felt happier than ever and free. She could appreciate herself for all that she'd been through. She learned to embrace her emotional bravery, and she liked who she was becoming.

To Do or Not to Do

1. Practice emotional bravery. In all situations you have what it takes to rise to the occasion, to apologize when you've blown it, to face what's troubling you, to cry, to smile and move forward.
2. Take care of your body. Try it all: massage, acupuncture, Rolfing.
3. Be happy that you are gaining so much experience. Experience is what turns us into wise women.
4. Stop running around like a headless chicken. Take a nap.
5. Set a gentle pace. Give yourself credit.

"Never regret.
If it's good, it's wonderful.
If it's bad, it's experience."

—Victoria Holt

Symptoms of Advancing Happiness...

> You spend more time at the local nursery buying plants than at the cosmetic counter buying makeup.
> You adore comfy shoes.
> You're beginning to notice birds.
> You're grateful that you have everything you need.
> One of your favorite pastimes is sitting and staring.

Quantum Leaps

Intuition is a woman's way of knowing. In the second half of life women's intuition is highly developed. It is a powerful and precious aspect of who we are. It makes us so intriguing. With intuition we can understand the unspoken, make a quantum leap, and go directly to the heart of the matter. We don't have to waste time reasoning things out; we can jump to a perfect conclusion without all the wrangling. A woman cannot say how she knows what she knows. She simply gets a hunch and responds.

I saw a guy on the noon news promoting healthy toothpaste. I was infatuated by his dapper style and his confident demeanor, so I called his headquarters in Chicago and left him a message. To my surprise, he called me back, and within a month he'd flown to Seattle to take me out. He wined and dined me, gave me a big carton of toothpaste, and asked me to be his West Coast salesperson or his wife. I declined both, but I learned a lot about following my intuition and enjoying the process.

Forty-three-year-old Daphne grew up in Atlanta and returned there after college to take a public relations job. She climbed the company's ladder, bought a house, and turned it into a showpiece with magnificent gardens. She had a full life with friends and family, but she sensed there was something more for her to experience. One evening over drinks with her girlfriends she dropped the bombshell: "I am moving to Seattle." She was as shocked to hear the news as her girlfriends, who didn't fully believe her until they saw the For Sale sign in the front yard.

After the move, wonderful things happened to Daphne. That's what happens when we follow our intuitions. Daphne took a landscaping class at the community college. She couldn't believe her luck! Not only did she meet a man in that class whom she eventually married, but she made a connection with a woman who introduced her to an owner of a firm that handled marketing and publicity for gardening and landscape companies. Daphne's experience in public relations, combined with her passion for landscaping, landed her the job of her dreams after only two and a half months in town. It was her intuition, however, that put her in the right place at the right time.

Life is a mystery and there are many dimensions to it. There are many unseen forces in the universe working on our behalf. To ignore our intuitions is folly. Life would be so flat without them.

Some folks claim that life is simpler if we blot out all our perceptions and live by the facts. "Just the facts, ma'am," they say. We midlifers know that making decisions based on a prescribed way of doing things is mechanical and that it doesn't necessarily lead to satisfaction. Life is a mystery and there are many dimensions to it. There are many unseen forces in the universe working on our behalf. To ignore our intuitions is folly. Life would be so flat without them.

As we age, we need our intuition more than ever. With so many changes, fads, technical advances, digital gadgets, and newfangled thingamajigs it's easy to feel as if we are becoming obsolete. But with our intuition in good working order, we will be able to stay true to our own path. It is our intuition that will guide us through. As we age, we are more concerned with how the universe works than with our cell phone, flat screen television, or the latest digital device. Even though reality TV rules the airwaves, there is something much more entertaining! We can turn off the television and turn on intuition. Intuition goes way beyond reality. Our intuitions are the sweet nudges that take our breath away and leave us in wonderment.

To Do or Not to Do

1. To the single ladies: Watch the noon news for smart, dapper guys and give them a jingle.

2. Keep your intuition in good working order. Start by paying very close attention to your hunches and be aware of what they are telling you.

3. Keep track of what happens when you follow your intuition. Share the outcome with others. Your stories will encourage them to develop their own intuition.

4. Tell the youngsters about intuition, unseen forces, and how the universe works.

5. Get a young person to help you with your digital devices and thingamajigs. They are very adept with technical equipment.

"Life seems simpler if we blot out awareness of its mystery,
but such a life is an impoverished one."

—SISTER WENDY

Getting Dirty

Have you noticed how many women above forty-five are into gardening? These days, it seems like everybody in middlescence is doing it. Bella has found a highly inventive way of going about it. On her fiftieth birthday she threw herself a garden party. The invitations read: Dress for digging in the dirt. Your birthday gift to me is helping me plant a garden. Please join me on Saturday for my first annual garden party plant-a-thon and brunch.

Not everyone was into gardening so a few folks didn't show up, but the eight of us who did put on our gardening gloves, sun visors, and knee pads, planted a fabulous vegetable garden. The work was hard and satisfying—pulling weeds, moving dirt, wielding shovels and rakes and hoes.

After our digging was done, Bella served a gourmet brunch that knocked our socks off. Party pepper shrimps, Caesar cream on parmesan toast, crunchy glazed pecans, and rosemary biscuits. And the smorgasbord didn't stop there. Bella served her infamous crab and asparagus quiche, strawberries with chocolate-hazelnut cream, blueberry pie, and enough champagne and vodka punch to make even the weariest of gardeners giddy. Even though the only gardening I do is in pots, after that garden party, I could testify to the abundant gratification that came from getting my hands dirty.

Gardening really is a metaphor for all of life. Nurturing growth is what women do. Protecting the ones we love, being patient, watching the little ones grow and bloom. Like all flowers in the garden, all of us are really very fragile. At our age, we understand that seasons change and at midlife we know that we're launching a new phase.

"I'm glad to be forty," Marla says, and now that she is into gardening, she can attest to how much fun she is having. She isn't as picky as she once was about keeping her house tidy. "Life is becoming too short to bother with the details of dusting and mopping that used to hang me up." Marla is landscaping the back acre and she is bending acacia tree branches into fences. "That fence is a work of art," her neighbor pointed out. "Score one for me," Marla says, "cuz I was just having fun."

Fun isn't about doing a particular activity. Fun is an attitude, a way of looking at the world, a state of mind.

Fun isn't about doing a particular activity. Fun is an attitude, a way of looking at the world, a state of mind. Fun at forty comes in new ways and one of them is in the garden. That's the pleasure of hanging out with flowers, pulling weeds, and getting dirty.

"Digging in the dirt keeps me grounded," Annie says. She lives in a high-rise building, but that doesn't stop her from gardening. Every spring she rents a pea patch in the city and begins preparing the soil for planting. She plants everything in that square patch—lavender, tomatoes, petunias, and corn. During the summer she goes there every evening to water and talk to her "babies." She met Tim there. He was the gentleman widower two plots away. They spent all summer digging in the dirt together. They have plants in common. Throughout the winter their friendship kept growing, just like his prize pumpkins from last fall. Annie told me she can't wait to spend another summer having fun and getting dirty.

Word about the party and the pea patch is spreading. Bella is already getting calls begging for next year's invitation. By sixty, Bella's garden is probably going to be a showstopper. I'm definitely attending. And Annie, well, she is getting calls too. All us single gardeners want to know if farmer Tim has any brothers.

To Do or Not to Do

1. Loosen up on housework. Spend the day in the garden instead.
2. Dig in the dirt. Follow Bella's party theme and invite folks to plant your garden.
3. Bend branches into atrellis, tie them with jute, and plant a climbing rose bush.
4. Single gardeners take notice: Rent a pea patch in the city and look for a gentleman farmer.
5. Bake a blueberry pie! See the following recipe.

1. Cook on top of stove until thick:
   ½ cup sugar
   3 Tbsp. cornstarch
   1 tsp. cinnamon
   1 tsp. butter
   1 tsp. nutmeg
   1 Tbsp. frozen orange juice concentrate

2. Cool slightly and then add:
   2 cups fresh blueberries and ½ cup slivered almonds
3. Pour into a graham cracker crust.
4. Serve with vanilla ice cream or whipped cream.

"It's difficult to think anything but pleasant
thoughts while eating a home-grown tomato."

—LEWIS GRIZZARD

Rent-A-Monk

In need of prayer or guidance? Having trouble getting in touch with your inner spirit? Have no fear—now you can rent a monk. I'm not kidding! There really is such a service. The "monk" is Dr. Cat, a counselor, a shamanic practitioner, and an ordained minister. Dr. Cat offers a personalized, daily prayer support service called Rent-A-Monk.

For a small fee, Dr. Cat will pray for you, your friends, your family, and even your animals. Rent-A-Monk service is an ingenious way to get the attention of the unseen forces in the universe and get them working on our behalf. Studies show that prayer makes a difference for the sender as well as the receiver. The way I see it, with all the transitions and upheavals going on in us and around us, the more positive vibrations in the air, the better.

Rent-A-Monk even comes with a money-back guarantee, so you have nothing to lose. The one and only time I bought antiwrinkle cream, there was no guarantee at all and I didn't see any improvement. But with Rent-A-Monk, Dr. Cat is very devoted, and if she commits to pray you can rest assured that she will follow through. "I'm a monk in the material world," she says.

Prayer is fuel for the soul, a medium of connection that opens our hearts and keeps us humble. We've done all that we can do and now we need help from a higher power. By the time we hit middle age we've prayed plenty, even if we don't realize it.

When we're young and naïve, our prayers are often full of desires, wants, and pleadings. Those harmless requests are the beginnings of our awareness of a benevolent force greater than ourselves. When we pray, we're asking for guidance and a helping hand. We're acknowledging that we're vulnerable. As we mature, we understand how vulnerable we really are, and our prayers take on the spirit of a grateful heart.

When Suzanne's house caught on fire, her prayers were ones of thanksgiving that no one was hurt. "Instead of making requests like I did when I was younger," Suzanne says, "now I'm grateful that my family is healthy and happy because that is all I really need."

> We have much to be grateful for, but sometimes we get so caught up in the day-to-day grind of household duties—and the useless game of trying to stay forever young—that we forget to count our blessings.

We have much to be grateful for, but sometimes we get so caught up in the day-to-day grind of household duties—and the useless game of trying to stay forever young—that we forget to count our blessings. "I'm blessed with a naturopath who gives me herbs instead of hormones," Suzanne says, "a massage therapist who smoothes out the kinks in my neck, and a personal trainer who pushes me beyond what I thought I could achieve."

So whether you use Rent-A-Monk, pray by yourself, or start your own prayer club, perhaps you might want to incorporate Suzanne's two guidelines for prayer:

1. Ask and Receive. Ask for what you need and be grateful for what you receive.

2. PUSH, which means "Pray Until Something Happens."

To Do or Not to Do

1. PUSH (Pray Until Something Happens).
2. Enlist the services of Rent-A-Monk at *www.dract.org*, and if you like it you might want to consider starting your own prayer service.
3. Acknowledge your middle-age aches and count your middle-age blessings.
4. Pray for those you know and love, and even those you don't!
5. Be assured that we are all grateful to you for your prayers.

"Dear Lord, So far today, I am doing all right.
I have not gossiped, lost my temper, been grumpy, greedy, nasty,
selfish or self-indulgent. I have not whined, cursed, or eaten any
chocolate. However, I am going to get out of bed in a few minutes
and I will need a lot more help after that."

—ANONYMOUS

Always Be More Loving

Leigh is dealing with tremendous loss. She hasn't been the same since her friend Jill died of breast cancer.

"Jill's death broke my heart," Leigh says. "I realize now I'm closer to the end of my life than I am to the beginning." Since her friend's death, Leigh is putting her energies into new things—getting and keeping up has lost its meaning. At forty-four she's asking herself, "What's important to me?"

That's how death is; until it touches us up close and personal, we don't think much about it. We're busy living out our destiny and biology.

Our primary concern is with exploring our newfound strengths and all those sensations. We are concerned with doing the sex, romance, reproduction dance. We are focused on raising our families and getting ahead.

> Until death touches us up close and personal, we don't think much about it. We're busy living out our destiny and biology. We are concerned with doing the sex, romance, reproduction dance. We are focused on raising our families and getting ahead.

Then a friend gets cancer, a parent dies, or a tragedy hits, and we are shaken to our core. It happened to Leigh. It happened to me when William, my sweetheart for ten years, was told that he had a malignant tumor.

They say that when you die your life flashes before your eyes. But it's more than that—your life can flash before you when you lose a friend or loved one as well. The year that William died I lived with death, and I certainly reviewed the shape and texture of our ten years together. In doing so, I came to the conclusion that we were doing the best we could and that the only thing that mattered was to be more loving—always to be more loving.

And that's why Leigh is taking time off from her career. She wants to be closer to home and more available for her kids and husband. Leigh is not terrified by death. What terrifies her is not living fully. She's scared of succumbing to the chatter in her mind, that endless chatter that is calculating, scheming, making plans, and working out strategies. The chatter that says, *I can be happy when I have enough money in the bank, when the children are in college, when the house is paid for, or when I'm skinny.* The chatter that keeps us missing out on all the love that is available to give and receive—it makes us think too much and close down our hearts.

In rethinking her life, Leigh came to a realization about her relationship with her husband. "We only talk about the children. I hardly know him anymore except as a father." So to get a jump-start on reconnecting as a couple, she signed them up for a couple's massage class and a date once a week. He's willing.

Death is the backdrop that makes being alive so sweet. Death is coming for all of us. Everyone is dying and that includes our parents, our sweethearts, our children, our neighbors. We don't know when it's coming or who is dying first, but we do know that it is coming. If we love the people we love really well, then when the time to part comes, we will have no regrets. If we love one another beautifully, we will part beautifully. We will be thankful that life gave us so much.

To Do or Not to Do
1. Notice the chatter that says, "I'll be happy when . . ."
2. Have a little chat with yourself about what is important.
3. Say "I love you" to every person that you love.
4. Be loving. Always be more loving.
5. Throw your arms to the heavens and say, "I'm Alive!"

"The thing about happiness is that it doesn't help you to grow; only unhappiness does that."

—LANA TURNER

Quiet Little Hobbies

"Last week I made sugar water for the hummingbird feeder and instead of pouring it into the feeder I poured it down the sink—three times!" the Lady Bug Lady told me, laughing at herself. The Lady Bug Lady got her name because of her book club. One summer she had a continual swarm of lady bugs in her house and the moniker stuck. "That year all the hats, gloves, and scarves that I knitted had lady bugs on them," she recalls. This year, her logo is hummingbirds.

"As I get older I notice that I do less, accomplish less, and enjoy it more," she says. "I wake up at five in the morning, and by ten I've watered the petunias and lobelia on the deck. I've counted the hummingbirds and eavesdropped on the chattering crows." After that the Lady Bug Lady might go for a walk in the wetlands. She tutors a Russian woman in English, and if the weather is decent they study on a bench at the marina. "I need big doses of wind and fresh air to think clearly," says the Lady Bug Lady.

"Nature is my hobby," Tanya tells me as we look through her panoramic photographs. "Staring at mountains makes me happy." During the week Tanya works as a social worker in a hospital and on the weekends she goes hiking. "When I'm outdoors I'm one with the world, I'm thrilled and excited." She calls the mountains her pets. "Hi there, Mount Baker," she says. "You're my big, brave mountain." As she tells stories about her favorite rocks appearing new and raw next to the snow or as she describes the blueberries turning red, she slides into her fading Texas drawl. "Oh, cute little rock," Tanya says, or, "I adore those sexy colonies of lacy, polka dot mushrooms." And when she tells you that she goes "wild over hunky, leafy maples" and that "eagles are my buddies," she makes these statements with such dramatic feeling that you fall in love, too. The woods is her sacred place. There isn't a sound to disturb her and that becomes her temple.

Jean is thrilled by fabric. With a little leftover ribbon and wrinkled paper, with a spare bead and an old button, Jean magically transforms a drab box into a treasure. With a twist, a tassel, and braid, Jean becomes the queen of wrapping. Such a tiny gesture but filled with so much love.

"I quilt because it is the way that I access my spiritual world," Sagewauker says. "I love the colors of the fabric, the creativity of putting my design together, and the thoughts of whom this may be for." A registered nurse and director of a home health agency, Sagewauker has comforted hundreds of people and made dozens of quilts. "As I get my fabric out, as I cut it and sew it into a quilt, a movie of my life passes through my head. I let things pass by and then I get an inspiration." Quilting is her meditation. She finds God there.

Quiet little hobbies are so exhilarating. Inspired by lady bugs and hummingbirds, rejuvenated by mountains, revived by our beloved ones, invigorated by fabric, reminisced over through quilting.

Quiet little hobbies are so exhilarating. Inspired by lady bugs and hummingbirds, rejuvenated by mountains, revived by our beloved ones, invigorated by fabric, reminisced over through quilting. As artists and creative midlifers we must consciously partake in quiet hobbies that nurture our spirit. We have to hang out with our muse, restore our soul, and walk among our nature companions. We need to tap in to our innocent zeal, rejoice, and lift our hands to the heavens. Oh what bliss to be awake, alive, and partaking in quiet little hobbies.

To Do or Not to Do

1. Ask yourself, What is your quiet little hobby?
2. What inspires you? Don't wait for your friends to do it with you. Do it by yourself.

3. Walk in nature. Talk to mountains. Hug trees.
4. Design your own logo. Use it on your very own creations.
5. Wrap boxes and turn them into presents. Cut fabric and design quilts. Comfort one another.

"So you see, imagination needs moodling—long, inefficient, happy idling, dawdling and puttering."

—Brenda Ueland

Coming Clean

Pat has done a lot of living and a lot of bathing.

She takes one bath in the morning, one before she goes out in the evening, and another one before she goes to bed at night. Pat lives a big life and that requires lots of bathing. "You are the cleanest woman I have ever seen," her third husband, the doctor, used to tell her.

Pat gets into her bathtub for all occasions. It's a calming ceremony for coping with the magnitude of her life. She's had three husbands. She divorced the first, buried the second and the third. She's been a single mother of two children and the stepmother to four. She's watched over a half a dozen dogs and a half a dozen men in between. She plants so many flowers that the neighbors come over to peek at her garden. She's danced at her children's weddings and attended the funerals of her parents, grandparents, husbands, and very dear friends. She's cooked as many meals as there are stars in the sky, lived in a half a dozen houses, thrown a couple hundred parties, had several careers, and now she's selling real estate.

And she celebrates it all in her tub. In the bath, she cries over the victories and defeats. She splashes, gossips, and celebrates from there too. "I have a phone by my bathtub. I visit with my friends and have philosophical conversations that might go on for hours. I'm off the clock in my tub."

Water is healing, and all life depends on it. It's the basic element in our bodies. It has no form; it's infinitely adjustable, fluid, and moving. We rely on water and water is a metaphor for how we all must learn to be—unrigid, unfrozen, and flowing. Water remains pure and clear if it moves and flows. It becomes cloudy if it remains stagnant. Unconsciously, Pat must know thati because she's diligent about moving, learning, and growing. She's explored the latest human potential movements—from body work, rebirthing, mystery schools, encounter groups, psychotherapy, mentors, spiritual teachers, and wise counsel. "I do it to evolve and become more fully human. I thought most people were a little stuck and I didn't want to end up like that." Bathing is her stress reduction. "I wash away all the negative energy, smoking, coughing, germs, and negative comments," she says. "It neutralizes my energy field. I've had perfect health, I rarely get a cold, I don't take medication, and I sleep seven hours, right through the night."

 "No one, and I mean no one, gets into my bed without taking a bath first."

Pat is queen of bathing, a connoisseur of French soap, bubbles, fresh smelling salts, lotion, fuzzy slippers, fluffy robes, soft gigantic towels, candles, and low light. "Some people may think I'm neurotic," she says, "but no one sleeps in my bed unless they've taken a bath." When her grandkids come over they know the routine and happily jump in to swim and play. Pat draws a bath for all her overnight visitors, "No one, and I mean no one, gets into my bed without taking a bath first."

To Do or Not to Do

1. Add three baths to your daily routine. Tell anyone who objects that it's either a bath or Prozac.

2. Follow this ritual for good health:
   Wake up, work out, and take a bath.
   Go to work, come home, and take bath.
   Go out for the evening, come home, and take a bath.
   Go to bed and sleep well.

3. Stock your bathroom with bubbles, soaps, salts, oils, candles, fluffy robes, gigantic towels, music, and a telephone.

4. Never let anyone into your bed unless they've taken a bath.

5. Go with the flow, stay flexible, learn something new, and keep swimming.

"My recipe for health?
Water, sleep, and self-acceptance."

—DANA REEVE

Little Freedoms . . .

> You are refining your taste for the finer things—fresh air, full moons, and flowers.

> You prefer making peace with your relatives over being right.

> You prefer to give and receive experiences in place of presents.

> You focus more on where you are than where you have been.

> You say "I love you" easily.

Section Six . . .

ON NOT
Taking Yourself So Seriously

Aren't we funny? We are pieces of work—pieces of artwork not yet completed. And that's a good thing. Why would we want to be complete? Life is art. Art is an alchemical process, more magic than science. We may not be as young as we once were, but we know now how sexy and cute we were back then. We know now the sensual women we've become. We know now that sensuality depends less on cuteness and more on coming to our senses. We are letting go of fear, anger, and resentment. We are becoming more magnificent—softer and funnier. Laughter and middlescence go together. The more difficult our situation, the more we need laughter. There are so many cosmic jokes flying around that if we are serious, we will miss them all. We do not want to do that.

The Smiling Turtle Pose

We don't realize that we have arrived at middlescence until we unexpectedly see our reflection in a mirror. We imagine that we look exactly like we did in our twenties and thirties, then we catch a glimpse of our face in the mirror. What we see can be quite shocking.

Gabrielle caught a glance of herself in the passenger-side rearview mirror of her car and saw an unfamiliar face staring back. "Yikes there's an old woman in the rearview mirror!" she shrieked to her husband, Jeff, who was at the wheel. "Do I look old, honey?" Gabrielle tilted her chin upward, slanted her head an eighth of an inch to the right. Maybe if she could get just the right angle she'd look like her younger self. It didn't work, the woman staring back still looked fifty-nine and now slightly lopsided.

I'm starting to look like a grandmother, Gabrielle thought. She was a grandmother and adored her grandchildren, but that didn't mean she wanted to look grandmotherly. *Don't worry, Gabrielle,* she told herself, *those rearview mirrors distort things and make things appear closer.* To convince herself that she didn't yet look her age required emergency maneuvers.

Several years previous, an acquaintance, a minor celebrity named Scarlet, had taught Gabrielle a trick that takes years off when posing for the camera. According to Scarlet if you sit straight up, put shoulders squarely back, hold your chin up and stick your neck outward farther than the fullest part of your breasts, you'll look tightly drawn and tense. According to Scarlet tightly drawn and tense is better than looking saggy. "Make like a turtle, stick your neck out," Scarlet instructed her. In this position your double chin disappears and creases in your neck smooth out. Smile, but don't squint your eyes because that makes crow's feet more prominent. Open your eyes wide, but not so wide that they appear froglike or buggy.

"Everything looks better when I'm smiling. I wash my face smiling and I put on lipstick smiling, because if I don't have a grin on my face I look angry."

Gabrielle's been practicing the turtle stance for at least a year. "Whenever I look in the mirror I stick my neck out and smile," she says. "Everything looks better when I'm smiling. I wash my face smiling and I put on lipstick smiling, because if I don't have a grin on my face I look angry."

Why don't I want my age to show? Why do we dismiss older women?
Gabrielle asks herself. Denial takes effort and even the turtle attitude
can't push away reality.

Gabrielle's sixtieth birthday is around the corner, and the age thing
is coming at her from all directions. "I've been guilty myself of dismissing the elderly," Gabrielle admits. "There's this withered person
wrapped in a bundle of wrinkles in my gym class who I'm sure has so
much to say, but I don't even bother talking to her. I don't know why. I
guess I assume she'll only talk about arthritis, and I don't want to hear
about that."

Even with the turtle pose we can't ignore that age is showing, and
that's when panic sets in. We all grouse about our aging faces. When
we catch a glimpse of ourselves in the mirror, we know that aging is
not far off—it's here. We're guilty of dismissing the elderly even though
that's who we are quickly becoming. "I'm trying to love my aging face,"
Gabrielle says. "Even if there is agony in it?" I ask. "There is an honesty
to agony," she says. "It clears the eyes."

To Do or Not to Do

1. Don't make age the issue. Tell yourself, I'm doing great instead
   of, For my age I'm doing great.
2. Practice the turtle pose. Look in the mirror, stick your neck
   out, and smile.
3. Take care of your health. After all, it's freedom from illness
   that determines the length and quality of life.
4. Imagine yourself happy and elderly. What will you be? What
   will you be doing?
5. Make conversation with the elderly. What goes around comes
   around and maybe some youngster will talk to you too.

"You can't go forward looking in a rearview mirror."

—Tammy Faye Bakker Messner

To Dye or Not to Dye

I have sacrificed and suffered over the years for good hair. Haven't we all?

I volunteered for my first permanent wave when I was ten years old. My mother thought that curls would be easier to maintain than my straight, thick locks, but my hair turned into such a frizzy, brittle mess that I refused to let her touch my head after that.

But the torture didn't stop there, I confess. I have slept on rollers the size of rolling pins. I have written term papers while sitting under steamy, hot, plastic bubble hair dryers. I have scalded my scalp with hot rollers and curling irons. I have colored my hair raven black and had it turn blue. I have colored it red and had it turn orange. I once agreed to let my hairdresser cut my hair to look like Twiggy's. Problem was that I was not skinny like Twiggy. My hair was so lopsided and out of proportion to my body that I had to wear a scarf for two months to avoid my boyfriend's laughter. I have poked my scalp with bobby pins, steel combs, and barrettes. I have used industrial strength glue to attach ribbon. I have split my ends with rubber bands and nylon brushes. I have spent a fortune on phony ponytails and fake wiglets. I have lugged a backpack stuffed with hair equipment—sprays, shampoos, and blow dryers—through Europe.

Fortunately, at my age, I can finally afford to stay in hotels that provide such necessities. Still, hair anguish continues. As we grow older, there is one burning question on all of our minds: Do we color our hair, or do we go gray gracefully?

As we grow older, there is one burning question on all of our minds: Do we color our hair, or do we go gray gracefully?

We girls over forty have to stick together. It's far too easy to fall victim to the youth culture and make a *very* bad hair decision. Sure, we can listen to what the perky twenty-year-old hairdresser recommends, but when it comes down to it, we decide whether to color, cut, grow, curl, or spike it up. We've suffered for women's rights, fought for the right to vote, and we must continue to demand our inalienable right to decide the fate of our hair.

We make the decision: to dye or not to dye.

We've suffered for women's rights, fought for the right to vote, and we must continue to demand our inalienable right to decide the fate of our hair. We make the decision: to dye or not to dye.

So the question remains—do we dye our locks to suit our current fancy or let them turn gray?

Sure, we can gather feedback from our friends and family, but when it comes right down to it, each of us has to stand in front of the mirror, look directly into the face of the "older" woman staring back, and make the decision. There's no right or wrong answer. It's a matter of personal preference. As grown-up girls we will not shirk this duty. We will step up to the mirror and be responsible. It's a decision we must make absolutely alone.

Cicely has dyed her hair every color you can possibly imagine. She does it herself most of the time, but occasionally she's a walk-in. Last fall, when she showed up to her bridge group with the worst case of fake blond straw, her friends took her straight back to the hairdresser and pleaded with her never to do that again. "I dye, but I never know what color I will be from month to month," Cicely says. "But I don't mind because I've been told I have a cornucopia of personalities anyway."

"Dye, dye, dye or frost, frost, frost." is Lynda's motto. "Au naturel is fine for a lot of things—but not for my hair."

"I choose not to dye," Chloe says. "My hair is not a high priority, and this way my upper and lower are a matched set!" she says with a smile. I just wash and shake."

Once we start coloring our hair, we're trapped, and according to Marlena, "It's a bitch to stop." Her shoulder-length hair is dark, but her roots are salt and pepper. She would like to grow it out, but according to her hairstylist the only solution is to go for a buzz cut. Marlena has to cut off her flowing tresses to a half an inch; otherwise there will be a line of demarcation as it grows out, and that will take a couple of years to get rid of. Yikes!

We burned the bra for freedom, but once we discover how to revert to our natural gray without suffering through growing it out, we will all be free at last. Ask hairdressers for their advice on stopping the endless cycle of coloring, and they'll stare at you blankly. It's a beauty industry conspiracy. Eventually we will put a woman in the White House, and surely by then we can move forward with a dignified plan to turn gray.

To Do or Not to Do

1. Elect a woman to the White House! She will understand the real issues facing women.

2. Take charge. Write instructions for your stylist on a 3" × 5" card and take them with you. That way when you're sitting in her chair and at her mercy you can refer to them. They will keep you on track.

3. Remember, you can change your mind or hair color as much as you want.

4. Before you agree to the recommendation of your hairstylist, ask her if she would make the same recommendation to her own mother. Ask to see a picture of her mother before you agree.

5. If you do decide not to dye, spend the money you save on facials. You deserve it.

"Yes, we praise older women for a multitude of reasons. Unfortunately, it's not reciprocal. For every stunning, smart, well-coifed babe of seventy there is a bald, paunchy relic in yellow pants making a fool of himself with some twenty-two-year-old waitress.
Ladies, I apologize for all of us."

—ANDY ROONEY

Griping and Gratitude

"How's it going?" my friend Ragini asked. "I'm overwhelmed and underinspired," I answered. It was one of those days when I had too much to do. My book *Single* had just come out. I had three radio interviews scheduled, a full day of clients, and an evening speech. The manuscript deadline for this book was a week away. I was on the edge and tired. I took a deep breath and rambled off my complaints. Ragini listened, paying very close attention to what I was expressing. "I'm exhausted," I said, "and brain dead. I can't think of anything brilliant to say. I have no more sentences to write." Ragini nodded as I went on about all the commitments that were weighing me down. "There, that's it," I sighed. "That's a lot," she said. "I know I have nothing to gripe about," I said apologetically, "because I love what I do and I'm so grateful to be doing it." "Griping and gratitude go together," she said.

I thought about that statement long after our conversation ended. It made sense. Griping and gratitude do go together. It's true. We may gripe but that doesn't mean we're not grateful. In fact, grumbling is like weeding the garden. Once those pesky weeds are gone, the flowers are freer.

Greta was just finishing up her last round of chemo for breast cancer when her sister, Helene, was diagnosed.

For a few days, Greta suffered in a fog of disbelief. "It wasn't fair," Greta said. "It didn't make sense." After the news settled, the sisters took action. Greta called her oncologist and scheduled Helene an appointment for a second opinion. Within a week the decision was made: Helene's treatment protocol was identical to what Greta had been through. Once again they would be there for each other.

It was one of those blessings that hurt. Of course Greta was glad to be able to be there for her sister and Helene was thankful too, but still, at times it seemed too much to bear, and the sisters were overwhelmed. "Why? Why? Why?" they asked. "Why did we both get cancer?" Neither one was feeling very positive. "I hate needles," Helene said. "I do not want to lose my hair. I do not have time for this."

They griped a lot about cancer to each other. They griped about the traffic jam on the way to the clinic, they griped about needles and medical procedures. But they were also very grateful. They were grateful to all the nurses, the doctor, and the receptionist for being so understanding. When anyone showed them any kindness or helped them in any way, they were deeply grateful. They were grateful to the waitress who gave them the corner booth, they were grateful they could share Chinese chicken salad, they were very grateful to have each other and come through it together.

Just because we are grateful to be alive doesn't mean we don't have grievances. Some of our very best role models, from Eleanor Roosevelt to Gloria Steinem to Jane Goodall, have made very big protests and accomplished great things because they spoke out. We can gripe about stresses, heartaches, and injustices. When we do, we know that we are pulling the weeds so that we can grow taller.

To Do or Not to Do

1. Gripe to your friend and notice how grateful you are to have a friend who listens. Do the same for her.
2. Turn your gripes into causes and make a difference. Folks will be grateful to you for speaking up.
3. Buy yourself flowers.
4. Share a Chinese chicken salad with your sister. If you don't have a sister, share one with your brother or someone who seems like one of the family.
5. Thank everyone who has helped you. Everyone! Be kind to all the people who are kind to you.

"The idea of strictly minding our own business is moldy rubbish. Who could be so selfish?"

—Myrtie Barker

Beauty Parlor Protocol

I was hit by lightning when I was fourteen years old, and I survived with only a burn on my ankle and a quirky personality. I was widowed at twenty-nine, remarried and divorced by thirty-four. I raised a daughter as a single mother. I have been a waitress, a saleslady in the men's underwear department, and a ticket lady in a rodeo ticket booth.

One summer I wore a hairnet and stood at a conveyor belt for twelve-hour shifts weighing spinach. I have been a social worker in a hospital emergency room, in a psychiatric hospital, and in a residential treatment center for delinquents. I have made chocolate-rolled whipped cream cake from scratch. I have given a speech to 1,000 people, written ten books, and appeared on *Oprah*. I have repaired my own garbage disposal, rewired a lamp, and mopped up after a mini flood. I have wallpapered ceilings, refinished furniture, and bargained with used car salesmen. I have been broke and dodged bill collectors. Once I even argued rationally and politely to an IRS auditor. In spite of those skills, I still am unable to consistently and coherently communicate my needs and wants to my hairdresser.

We agree that every woman has her own personality and needs a signature look to go with it, right? And we can agree that every woman needs a hairdo that isn't confusing, right? If we can agree on that, then certainly we can agree that our hair needs to match who we are *now*, not who we were a decade ago, right? If you've been wearing a beehive or a French twist since the 1960s or 1970s, then it's definitely time for an update, right?

Searching for a compatible hairstylist is harder than finding a soul mate.

Searching for a compatible hairstylist is harder than finding a soul mate. I've been convinced that I've found my match only to be disappointed with my cut or color months later. "I like to let it grow," I say. "Really?" she asks with a tone that suggests that I look better with a chin-length bob. "I'm thinking about adding some cool red streaks," I say. "Really?" she says. "Warm tones are softer." "I'm thinking about letting my hair go gray." "Really," she says. "Why would you want to do that?"

The first visit usually goes swimmingly, but after about six visits the understanding between us gets muddled. The stylist either gets lackadaisical and takes me for granted or I expect too much of her. We stop communicating and eventually we grow apart.

Leaving a hairdresser requires all the finesse I can muster. Goodbyes are painful. When it comes to changing hairstylists we find out just how low we can sink. We find out that we're not as grown up as we think we are.

"I've been known to stay with a hairdresser just because I didn't want to hurt her feelings," says Sadie. She once stayed with a bald, gay hairdresser because he had the most interesting gossip. But he was known for calling up clients and asking why they cancelled their appointment. After that terrifying experience, Sadie developed beauty parlor protocols.

Here are her protocols:

1. Beg. If you see a hairstyle or color that you like, do whatever you have to do to get that stylist's name and where she works. Once you are sitting in her chair, again, do whatever it takes to get her home phone number. You need to know her whereabouts at all times. Hairdressers mysteriously change salons, and you don't want her to slip out of sight.

2. If you find a hairdresser who gave you just the right color, extract the color formula from her by any means necessary. Make up some story about traveling to Indonesia and needing to inform the hairdresser there on color techniques.

3. Have a backup stylist. A lot of people feel like they're cheating if they do this, but Sadie thinks it's imperative. She suggests handling this by being honest with both. Say something like, "You're so busy that I had Millie cut my hair

last month." Then add a compliment or reassurance: "I'm glad our schedules matched this month." If you're honest, your stylist will understand that her hours and location are not always convenient for a busy woman like you.

4. Be friendly, but don't become buddy-buddy. That makes it too awkward when they raise prices and you decide to go elsewhere.

5. Never choose a hairdresser within twenty miles of where you buy your groceries or go to dinner. That's because when you do change from one to another, which of course you will, you won't want to run into them at the supermarket and have to make up some excuse. Warning: Stylists in the same area tend to know each other, and if you switch too often they probably know what you're up to. In the worst-case scenario they might blackball you. It's best to acknowledge your habits up front. Announce on the second visit, "Nothing against you, but I am a switcher."

6. Answer this question: Do you like the way your hair looks when you leave the salon? It seems that most women, after spending hundreds of dollars for a cut and color, go straight home and puff it up and brush it out. If you like your hair right after it's done, book another appointment instantly.

Our hairstylist is vital to our infrastructure. We hate to admit it, but we know it's true. We can't get along without one. By middlescence we know that it takes a whole team of people to keep us running smoothly and looking good. Our hairdresser is a member of that chosen few—gynecologists, dermatologists, manicurists—who keep us together. That is why we must learn the protocols and communication techniques to interface with all of them. What *would* we do without them?

To Do or Not to Do

1. Update your resumé. List all your personal skills, every job you have ever held, every minor and major accomplishment. Reviewing your life in this way might give you courage to talk directly to your hairdresser.

2. Check out the hairdresser's hair. Her personality is not as important as her hair.

3. Choose a stylist with a name that resonates on a spiritual level with you. For example, my hairdresser this year is Zoey. When I told my best friend Jean that I was changing to her, she said, "I am drawn to this woman, too, because Zoey is the name I plan to give to my next dog or cat. I think this might be a good sign."

4. Make friends with your flaws but don't point out your age spots or your varicose veins to the other patrons. Those things are private and only for your masseuse to know.

5. Send me the name of your favorite stylist in case I visit your city.

—————

"The truth is that I really like the ease with which I move through the world right now, but I wouldn't mind being cute just one more time."

—Suzy Kellett

Eloquent Riddles

If anyone proves that less is more it's Vedika, a walking, talking meta-phor who affirms that the theory is true. She lost twenty pounds last year and she's more herself at fifty-three years old than ever, a tiny renaissance lady at 110 pounds. If you want to understand Vedika you have to be willing to play. You have to be silly and absolutely earnest. You have to put aside ideas of how a conversation should be and frolic with her in the moment. "It's a creative world," she says, "and we're all creative." If you have lunch with Vedika, take one of her classes, or attend a salon, you're signing up to dabble in "the amusement park for the soul." Her treatise, "The Creative Crack," is filled with riddles. "Nobody's watching," she instructs her students. "Paint like a child," she inspires. "Creativity arises from the unknown," she says. "If you know what you're doing, you've done it before." Explaining the unex-plainable is what Vedika is all about.

"Life is brutal and merciful at once," she says. Her partner, Mique—a stocky guy seven years older—died. Five months later she met August—a tall, lanky guy thirteen years younger—and a year after Mique's death, they were together. "Life hammered me with Mique's death and then gave me this wonderful gift of a man named August. Winter and summer at the same time." In grief and in love simultaneously.

That's what I mean about Vedika. She accepts whatever is going on as meaningful, mysterious art. "I'm a mystic," she announces in the middle of eating a pastrami sandwich. "I'm relentless in my pursuit. I'm curious. I want to know about the mystery."

"What's the mystery?" I ask.

"If we knew that, it wouldn't be a mystery," she answers.

"This is profound!" I'm thinking. Later when I'm home reconstructing our conversation I realize you had to be there. Taking words out of context sucks the energy right out and leaves them flat. Understanding from afar isn't as good as taking it in first hand. I can't explain Vedika from a distance. No, to take Vedika in, you have to be there. That's true about midlife transitions, too, and everything creative, isn't it? We have to slow down, not think too much, and be present to soak up all the nuances.

According to Vedika, we make up a lot of stories about what's going on when really we don't know for sure. Our stories trap us and keep us experiencing the world in the same prescribed way. That's not creative, that's not fun, and it keeps us limited by who we've told ourselves we are. Perhaps that's what a midlife crisis really is—an opening, a crack in the stories we've been telling ourselves. Maybe that's why wise people say, "The older I get the less I know." Maybe that's why at midlife we get very interested in resurrecting parts of ourselves that we have pushed aside.

Vedika is a poet, a philosopher, a mystic, a muse. "Creativity is surrendering," she says, "and making art is like lovemaking, you have to get yourself out of it and subject yourself to the mystery."

Perhaps that's what a midlife crisis really is—an opening, a crack in the stories we've been telling ourselves. Maybe that's why wise people say, "The older I get the less I know."

"Surrender, let go, and make way for the midlife juices to flow!" I say.

Vedika doesn't cook much, but when she does she views it as an art form. Her specialty is big pots of spaghetti sauce. She hates being overwhelmed by messes so she keeps her home in perfect order. For example, she would never have to-do lists. Vedika doesn't like pending. "I pay my bills immediately. I don't like anything hanging over me," she adds. "The more present I am, the less there is to do." I don't exactly understand what she means by that, but I'm not bothered. I'm enjoying the sunshine, the lunch, and our philosophizing. Who cares about what she means when I'm having such a good time?

Oh, one more thing that Vedika says, "The studio isn't only a physical space, it is also a state of mind. It is an open-ended laboratory where anything can happen. A mysterious cooking pot, a chemistry set, an altar." Isn't that brilliant? "Ahh!" I say. "Midlife is brimming with riddles."

To Do or Not to Do

1. Pay bills immediately and don't get trapped by pending.
2. Participate! Spin eloquent riddles, pursue the mysteries, and hang out with the questions.
3. Erase and rewrite the worn-out labels that you've been wearing.
4. Invite a muse or a mystic to lunch, buy them a pastrami sandwich, and get ready to romp.
5. Visit Vedika at *www.artsurgery.com* and tell her Judy sent you.

"Talent is like electricity.
We don't understand electricity, we use it."
—MAYA ANGELOU

You Are a Midlife Darling When . . .

> You walk into a room and sometimes can't remember what it was that you went in there for. You are not upset because you have things to do in there too.
> You have had a least one conversation this week about bodily functions, and it wasn't with a doctor.
> Good-looking guys call you ma'am.
> You are simplifying by giving away perfectly wonderful items from your closet.
> The dresses that you wore in your teens are back in style.
> You are stiff after sitting down, and when you get up it takes fifteen seconds or more to start moving.
> You don't eat after 6 P.M., and if you do you promise yourself never to do it again.
> Even though you own three or more pairs of reading glasses, you can never find even one pair when you're ready to read the newspaper.
> People frequently say, "You don't look that old," and you appreciate their kindness.
> You prefer a matinee movie to the late show.

Refine Your Stubborn Streak

Midlife is when you wake up one morning and the oldies playing on the radio are the ones you danced to in college. It's when the cute shoe salesman calls you ma'am, and when you begin noticing that your dentist, doctor, and lawyer are younger than you are. It's when you no longer understand the jokes on the late-night talk shows. It's when you don't know the names of the guests and do not care. No doubt about it, midlife can deflate your spirit more quickly than ice cream melting on the hot pavement, if you let it. To survive middlescence with your sense of humor intact, you're not only going to have to develop your funny bone, you're going to have to refine your stubborn streak. That part of you that doesn't want to and won't. You're going to have to be like the poet and artist Fryma who still refuses to paint realistically. Fryma is so determined about painting nude models in her own style that after seven years in painting class the teacher finally threw up her hands and said, "Go ahead and paint your own way."

Habe you ever done anything like that? Maybe you've gotten where you are by that obstinate resolve? Once you hit perimenopause you're going to need it—especially when it comes to communicating with your doctors and getting the care that is appropriate for you. Stubbornness serves a purpose. As a child it was that "I can do it myself" spirit that propelled your curiosity. As a teenager it defined you as separate from your parents and prepared you for the world, and maybe got you in some trouble. By middlescence a refined and polished stubborn streak is the determination that keeps you asking questions and finding answers.

If you've ever been called headstrong, pigheaded, opinionated, or obstinate you know what a daunting task it is to keep your will about you. With so many people going along with the crowd, it's enough to wear you down. As little girls we often got the message that we shouldn't be so stubborn. Take it from me, if you're over forty it's perfectly appropriate to revive that stubborn side.

> As little girls we often got the message that we shouldn't be so stubborn. Take it from me, if you're over forty it's perfectly appropriate to revive that stubborn side.

Perimenopausal and menopausal symptoms are sensitive personal matters, and if you don't address them in the way that fits for you, then you're left at the mercy of others' convictions. What suits your friends might not fit you. One friend may be using hormones while another swears by alternative treatments. The doctor's advice may be perfectly logical but that doesn't mean it will be compatible with your body. Without the ability to ask all the questions you have, it's easy to get sidetracked. In order to get the care you need, you might have to speak up, push hard, and say, "I don't understand," or "Nope, that's not for me," or "I'd like to think that over." It's up to you to consider the recommendations, sort through the information, take what fits, and leave the rest.

If you've been giving in to what others want for so long that you don't get around to thinking of yourself until there's ten minutes left in the day, it's definitely time to take a stand. The next time you have to go to the doctor, try dressing for the event in a way that makes you feel empowered—that expresses your wild, stubborn side. Fryma does. "Faux red hair paired with shades of red, pink, and orange clothes adds fire to being a painter and a poet," she says.

Next time you visit the doctor refuse to be interviewed wearing a paper gown or sitting on the examining table—it's distracting and it throws you off your game. Instead, tell the nurse in advance that you want to talk with the doctor in her office. Walk in there wearing your best stubborn gear—be it red plaid, pink polka dots, or orange stripes. The staff will understand that you are not only taking charge of your style, you are taking charge of your health. That is the purpose of our stubborn streak. To make sure our opinions are heard, that our needs are noticed, and that our concerns are addressed. As little girls we felt confused and bad when we were called stubborn, but now, at middlescence, we accept it as one of our many strengths.

To Do or Not to Do

1. Dress with flair for all your appointments. That includes doctors, accountants, lawyers, car mechanics. They will pay more attention if they think that you are eccentric, stylish, and your own person.

2. Dust off your stubborn streak and use it when you need to say no.

3. Ask as many questions as you need to. If you don't understand, ask until you do.

4. Practice saying, "Nope that's not for me" or "I'd like to think that over" as often as possible so that you'll be ready when you really need it.

5. When you are done at the doctor's office, put on oldies music for the drive home, melt into the groove, and let yourself go.

6. If and when you have grandchildren, never put them down for being stubborn. Tell them a few stories about your stubborn side. Play them some of your music.

"I've had heartaches, headaches, toothaches, earaches,
and I've had a few pains in the ass;
but I've survived to tell about it."

—DOLLY PARTON

"Art" Appreciation

I learned about my best friend, Jean's, secret aspirations while we were stuck in traffic next to a construction site. I think it was the construction workers that spurred her confession. You know, those guys with the hard hats wearing T-shirts with the rolled-up sleeves? As my Dad used to say, "I may be old, but I'm not blind." Jean and I can relate! We

d

ie face and a sculpted body just as much as the

wenties we couldn't look directly, we had to sneak sideways peeks. Three decades later, however, looking at a hot guy is
pure joy.

Jean says we have more fun looking at guys now than we did when
we were in our twenties. In our twenties we couldn't look directly, we
had to sneak sideways peeks. Back then, a mere glance was so intense,
brimming with excitement, assumptions, and ulterior motives, that you
could never look long enough. Looking at cute guys stirred things up and
led to complications that you may not have been seeking. Three decades
later, however, looking at a hot guy is pure joy. At our age we can gaze as
much as we like because the guys don't even notice that we're watching.
We're not flirting; our only intention is to appreciate. It's like spending
the day in Florence. Admiring Michelangelo's *David* doesn't mean you
want to ship him home and stand him in the garden. We don't want to
start anything—Jean's happily married and I don't date young—but we
both relish fine art. A young guy wouldn't even suspect that two women,
old enough to be his mother, are looking at him, so no harm done. For us,
it's like window shopping or spending the afternoon in the Louvre.

So there we are, two intelligent, successful women, mothers of
adults, patiently waiting and watching as the hot-blooded, drop-dead
gorgeous flagman directs us through the construction site.

"I want to drive a backhoe,." Jean blurts out.

"You want to drive a what?" I ask.

"I'd like to climb up on that backhoe, pull the levers, push the
buttons, and forge through the dirt."

"You like moving dirt?" I ask.

"It's not the dirt that inspires me," she says, "it's operating big machinery."

"You want to operate big machinery?"

"I'd like to be skilled at making it do whatever it does," she says. "I want to take control of a really big tool."

> "It's not the dirt that inspires me," she says, "it's operating big machinery."

I know that sounds a little Freudian, but I don't think that's Jean's motivation. Jean appreciates machinery, just like she appreciates art and all God's creations. It's more about the thrill, the beauty, and the power. The thrill of being high up, of being in charge, and having your hands on the controls. "I'd settle for a tractor, if it's big enough," Jean says. "After all, it's the skill that I'm after."

Driving a backhoe is an unusual wish for a grandmother, and if you knew Jean you'd be surprised that such a sophisticated lady would have such a burning desire. Perhaps that's why they say never judge a book by its cover. Me, well, I'd like to make Jean's wish come true. I'd like to be her fairy godmother and put her in a backhoe. I intend to investigate this further, and as soon as this book is completed I'm going to go down to that construction site and talk to those guys. That's the advantage of being over thirty. Those guys will take my request seriously.

Young guys are quite respectful of older women. That's certainly been our experience with waiters. Jean and I have had some great encounters with the best-looking waiters in Seattle. We were served breakfast at Café Campagne by a waiter with the deepest blue eyes. He smiled, made small talk, and gave us the inside scoop on the menu. If we had been twenty, we would have been too nervous to soak up all his attention. We would have played coy. The waiter at Maximellain's was a real charmer. We swooned shamelessly over his French accent and he didn't mind. "Where are you from?" we asked. "Pairee," he answered. "Been here long?" "A year. I go to the UW." We may not have been that bold in our thirties. He told us everything. It made our hearts skip. We left him a generous tip. The whole world is an art gallery waiting to be enjoyed. When we stop and gaze long enough we can see how beautiful the world really is. We see that everything is art—from the Louvre, to construction sites, to waiters at the corner bistro. There is a lot of power in art—for both the artist and the admirer. Art transforms reality and I can really appreciate that!

To Do or Not to Do

1. Appreciate art in all its forms. Visit Florence, the Louvre, and a construction site.
2. Eat at good restaurants and talk to the waiters. Show appreciation for a handsome face, a sculpted body, and a friendly attitude by leaving a generous tip.
3. Repeat after my Dad, "I may be old, but I'm not blind." Look all you want.
4. Blurt out any of your unfulfilled aspirations and ask your girlfriend about hers.
5. Play fairy godmother to your friend and grant her wishes, if possible.

"I have always adored beautiful young men. Just because I grow older my taste doesn't change. So if I can still have them, why not?"

—Brigitte Bardot

Black Lace Makes Them Laugh

She seldom wears black to bed anymore, except if she's in the mood or he's in the mood, and then she slips into something lacy and low. She owns fishnets and she wears them on occasion for sentimental reasons of course. He is appreciative when she slips them on. It makes him feel the way he felt when they were doing it all night and all around the house. Black lace reminds him of his younger days, and that makes them both laugh.

They've been together twenty-some years and sex is still good, but softer somehow. It's joyful. That's why she wears the lace—he likes it and she likes the joy that comes with giving. She gets turned on seeing that she's turning him on.

They call it "high sex" or "old sex" or "married sex." It's the sex that basks in warm appreciation and is constantly and astonishingly harmonious. Sex for them now is about mutuality, laughter, being in sync, playing peekaboo, and doing something together. Their joy is in the delight of sharing an amazing journey.

Love play begins long before foreplay.

Their lovemaking is not confined to the forty-five minutes of sex. It does not begin when the lights go out. Love play begins long before foreplay. And it is not confined to the bedroom. The way they treat each other, the daily acts of kindness, the loving glances, the genuine consideration, the mutual respect—it is this that empowers their love.

The best sex comes from letting go of fixed goals, fixed ideas, tensions, fears, opinions, and judgments, as well as the habits of analyzing, of explaining everything, of making excuses, and of thinking you know best. When you let go, you are in a state of awareness of the moment—you aren't far away in your thoughts, you are not anticipating this or that, you are not lost in some abstraction. You are right here in the now, fully alert and present. Which feels great in and of itself. Then you can smell the coffee and the roses. It's in the "Ah, this!" moment, with all your mental gibberish out of the way, that you're in love again.

They say that sex can be as good after sixty-five as at eighteen. Those who know claim it's often better—more mellow and less driven, even though there isn't as much jumping around. One man of seventy offers, "I'm still going strong, and I've been interested in sex since I was five! I'm not good-looking, I'm not rich, I may be totally crazy, but I enjoy the ladies and they sure do seem to enjoy me. I'm still a sexual being, and I don't want anyone to forget it!"

But there's another opinion. A lady of seventy-eight told me, "One disappointing thing about sex is that when you finally get comfortable with it, you're too old to really enjoy it or you no longer have a partner. I mean you can still enjoy it if you can find a partner, but it does start looking a little childish." I guess it all depends on who you are talking to.

The intoxicating sex of young love is different from the kind of sex you have later on. The first few months, everything you do sexually is so urgent that it's like a matter of life and death. But later on, when you're not quite so keyed up, your lovemaking will have a different dimension, a different flavor—more relaxed and sweeter. It can bring tears to your eyes and melt your heart.

To Do or Not to Do
1. Blow kisses. Show affection. Collect hugs.
2. Rise to the level where your thoughts are positive.
3. Don't push yourself to think loving thoughts, but rather find

the level inside you where thoughts of love and caring already exist.

4. Keep black lace stockings in the back of the drawer just in case.

5. Keep your sense of humor; you're going to need it.

―――

"Wear a taffeta slip that who-o-shes and crackles when you move.
This makes men delirious. Rub your thighs together when you walk.
The squish-squish sound of nylon also has a frenzying effect."

―GAIL GREEN AND JEANNIE SAKOL

Old Age Avoidance Disorders

I've made a discovery. I'm going to be famous! I'll go down in history as the woman who diagnosed the obvious. I've discovered a new classification of psychiatric disturbances called Old Age Avoidance Disorders. I can't believe that the American Psychiatric Association hasn't addressed this mental illness, after all, they've investigated all kinds of other neurotic ailments. The DSM-IV manual describes a plethora of psychological disturbances ranging from the disorder of written expression, to pica (that's the eating of nonnutritive substances), to bipolar, to cannabis intoxication, to phase of life problems. Under the phase of life category the manual lists such transitions as entering school, starting a new career, and changes involved in marriage, divorce, and retirement. But never once does it mention the trauma of aging.

Considering how many people suffer from Old Age Avoidance Disorders, doesn't it strike you as a little odd that there's no mention of this in the diagnostic manual? You'd think that researchers, psychologists, and social scientists would be lining up to study and treat it. Based on my own research and experience, I think I've stumbled on the criteria to validate an Old Age Avoidance classification.

> There's a social stigma about aging. Vintage cars and vintage clothes are hip; vintage people are eyesores.

There's a social stigma about aging. Antique furniture is valuable, but not antique people. Vintage cars and vintage clothes are hip; vintage people are eyesores. People are afraid to see aging. There's even a name for this phobia: *gerontophobia*, the fear of old people or of growing old. That's why I'm taking up the cause. I want maturing to be as hip as it is to be young. Old Age Avoidance Disorders are psychological disturbances so prevalent that there needs to be a separate classification in the manual. There needs to be a protocol for its treatment.

Old Age Avoidance is sweeping the nation. Everyone is in denial. We all need treatment. The tell-tale signs of Old Age Avoidance begin to manifest sharply in the forties. There's a wide range of symptoms, from the obvious—a red sports car in the driveway—to the more obscure—lying about your age and believing it when someone says, "You don't look a day over thirty-four." Everyone is searching for the fountain of youth. I know women and men who are so deeply depressed about getting older that they jump from doctor to doctor for reassurance and Prozac. I know a gentleman who spent his children's college money on hair replacements. Gerontophobics are swarming the border from Arizona to Mexico for eye lifts, colonics, and anti-aging formulas. Up until now no one has diagnosed this condition, and although I'm not big on psychiatric labels, I have to point this out so that we can find a cure. Without treatment these ailments can lead to more chronic conditions, such as Bitter Old Lady or Nasty Old Man.

Aging is not a popular subject and I don't expect to get much publicity about my findings. News anchors are afraid of aging too. Who can blame them? Who wants to age? No one except maybe eighteen-year-olds who can't wait to be twenty-one. But after that, there doesn't seem to be anyone wishing to grow older. Twenty-nine-year-olds complain about turning thirty. Thirty-nine-year-olds get "sorry, you're old" cards. From then on the birthday cards are downright insulting.

The only people who are happy to be old and look forward to adding another year are wise women. Wise women understand that life is fleeting, and they've stopped trying to hold on to the past. Wise women honor themselves and the frailties of our universal condition. Wise women, experts in compassion and creating, are beacons of encouragement, shedding light on a natural process.

No one wants to die, but death is coming. Rather than keeping ourselves in denial about it, isn't it wiser that we learn how to accept all stages of the life cycle? Instead of pretending that we're younger, let's celebrate that we're older. We're alive. We're becoming our best selves. We're champions of the authentic. Facing our own mortality is not for the timid, and anyone who's doing it deserves our recognition. They are our elders. They lift our spirits. Just as children need loving adults to protect and guide them through adolescence, we, too, need our elders to guide us through the middle of life.

To Do or Not to Do

1. Spread the word about the wise elders in your community. They are your community's finest resource. Designate each of them as Elder Ambassadors.
2. Write your congressman, call the governor, and send a letter to the editor. Demand a National Respect Your Elders Day.
3. Boycott advertisers who use only teenage models. Tell

them we want to see a full spectrum of women. We want to see women whose experience, compassion, and wisdom are showing.

4. Join the cultural revolution. Interview the elders. They have fascinating stories to tell.

5. Stamp out Old Age Avoidance Disorders. Put a sign in your yard, wear a button, get a bumper sticker that says "Elders Are Hip!"

"I love being fifty—you don't have to prove anything to anyone anymore. It absolutely sets a woman free."

—TAMMY FAYE BAKKER MESSNER

Simple Signs of Approaching Maturity . . .

> The twinkle in your eye is beginning to show.

> Men with receding hairlines are attractive to you.

> You say, "Oh, well," without disappointment.

> You say, "I see what you mean," without being defensive.

> You're thinking about buying a bike, a pair of rollerblades, or a scooter.

Section Seven . . .

Wisdom Is Adorable

Wisdom is adorable. It is subtle, so you have to pay close attention. It's a twinkle in the eye, a spring in the step, a smile that comes straight from the heart. Wisdom is not slick, it is wrinkled from experience. Wisdom is fresher than knowledge. Wisdom does not come from learning, it comes from living and unlearning. Wisdom does not have much to do with what we know or what we own, it has to do with how much we have lived. It is the truth that transcends intellectual understanding. It is the genuineness that comes from weathering. Wisdom shines through the cracks, the imperfect lines, and the worn spots. It is simple, intimate, unpretentious, and humble.

Wisdom is not slick, it is wrinkled from experience.

Wise Women and Turning Points

Once you have been through a midlife crisis or two, you know that middle age predicaments are not so much emergencies as they are turning points. This is the time in our lives when we don't have to explain ourselves. We are letting go of what no longer serves us. We are beautiful—inside and out—and we accept compliments happily. "People often tell me how beautiful I am," sixty-nine-year-old Irene told me, "and I say, 'thank you so much.' When I was younger I'd point out my flaws." Women are creative, intuitive, and becoming wiser, funnier, and lighter every year. We know the truth when we hear it.

Women can expect to live to be ninety. That means we are living long enough to forget the name of our first husband. Women are at the forefront of a cultural revolution. Women are having babies in their forties, going back to school in their fifties, dating younger—women are doing it all! Millie is eighty-seven and she is traveling to India. "My kids and grandkids don't want me to go and I can understand why they are worried, but I promised to call home every other day." The pendulum is swinging. Our society is changing. The fastest growing segment of our population is the folks over sixty-five. "I still feel like a beginner," Millie says.

This is the essential truth. Middle age is more than hormone fluctuations—these are the years of expansion. Our intellects, spirits, and hearts are immense. We know where we've been and what it took to get here. We are sympathetic to other women's plights, less judgmental, and more forgiving. There is no challenge that women can't meet. We know that the purest awareness is when we somehow step out of our own way and allow the wisdom to come through. Every wise woman knows when this happens. She is in partnership with the Divine and that is the highest form of expression.

Women are passionately in love with the impossible. That's why you can't fool us much. We understand with our hearts, not our heads. "Instead of thinking about getting old, I think about why I am here," Millie says. "I study love. Love in all its forms is fascinating."

That is the way of women. To express love in all its forms. "I like exercise as long as it is outdoors," she says. She's taking up speed walking around the cul-de-sac. "I appreciate the freedom that the younger generation of women have. Women can be happy alone. We are very independent."

According to Millie the most satisfying stages of life are the later ones. That's when we reach our creative high. Millie silk-screens colorful scarves with blessings, symbols, and prayers. She ties them from trees and gives them as gifts. She developed the concept when she saw prayer flags on a trip to Katmandu. Millie says we get more creative with age because we are more relaxed with ourselves. And when we are relaxed with ourselves we become very wise. That's the pivotal point. We are wise. We can feel it. We know it. We accept it and share it.

To Do or Not to Do

1. Graciously accept all compliments. Give words of encouragement back.
2. Tie blessings scarves on trees.
3. Take up speed-walking.
4. Call home.
5. Live long, live creatively, and do the impossible.

"You do not have to be good. You do not have to walk on your knees for a hundred miles through the desert, repenting. You only have to let the soft animal of your body love what it loves."

—MARY OLIVER

Dance Can Save Your Soul

"Are you twins?" the lovely young girl behind the bakery counter asked my friend Antonia and I as we were ordering slices of chocolate and coconut cake to share. We were thrilled with her observation. No one's commented on our similarities before, but we recognize them in each other. We both have dark hair and prefer twirly dresses. We both wear small, round glasses. We both have gypsy souls. We both love to dance. She's danced all of her life; I long to dance more often.

"I created myself through dance," Antonia tells me. Antonia is the name she chose for herself at nineteen, the same age at which she darkened her hair. Patsy May was the name her mother gave her. Patsy May, a bleached platinum blonde, would not suit a flamenco dancer. Antonia recalls, "When I heard the click, click, click of the flamenco and saw the footwork, I wanted to learn and no amount of reason (you can't support yourself dancing) could sway me from it."

My heart breaks ever so slightly when Antonia speaks of her childhood—poverty, violence, and the fears that are brought to a child by such instabilities. She's certain that it was the dance that healed her and I believe it's so. Dance revived her body, mind, and soul. Antonia moved into a gypsy commune and studied with a flamenco master. She was on tour with Jose Greco by the age of twenty-three.

I've never seen her dance, but when she describes the ruffled *bata de cola*, the dress with a tail, and the castanets, I'm swept away, as if I'm sitting in the front row, watching my twin, and my heart beats faster. I can feel it. Dance takes you to a place inside your soul that you may have long forgotten.

Dance is joyful and poignant movement. "It makes no sense and it isn't practical," Antonia says. "I wouldn't be where I am today with the joy in my heart if I were a little less stupid." Antonia never gave a thought to how she was going to get by. "I never learned how to think about money," she says. "I'm dim-witted in that way. I should have thought about my future. But when your back is up against the wall," she says, "you look at the world differently. When your survival is threatened you don't worry about school or even what you're going to have for dinner. Your whole reality is tenuous so you have to create a distraction that matches in power." For Antonia, dance was her survival.

There are lots of things that don't work out. "Dance is no guarantee that you won't have loss or frustration, but devoting myself to it was worth it," Antonia says. After a debilitating accident that left Antonia unable to dance or teach, she went to a remote mountaintop to recuperate and study the essence of dance—the light moving through the trees, the crow circling in the sky. "I went to the mountain to pursue the spiritual life, to live a life off the grid, and regain my health," Antonia explains. All of life is her dance. "I hope people will dance on my grave when I'm buried."

When I'm with Antonia, I notice the world through the soul of a dancer. She says something brilliant like, "I believe the life force itself is a balance between positive and negative impulses. I channel the expression of dance through the depths of my experiences. Therefore I was able to be very 'up' when dancing because other parts of my life had been so 'down,' " and I say to her, "That's brilliant, Antonia, write it down. That could be a book," I say. That's the dance we're doing together. She speaks to me of dance, and I encourage her to write it down.

We may not move like we did when we were younger but the beat goes on.

Life is movement, life is dance, existence is mysterious. We may not move like we did when we were younger but the beat goes on. It's pulsating through our veins. We can sway with the trees, swirl with the wind, pivot in the rain. We can talk with each other about the mysteries and write our observances down. "I'm sixty-one, yet I have no idea what it means to grow older," Antonia says, "and I don't know what the word *older* means. I don't know what I'm supposed to feel. As long as there is life I'll still dance. If in many years from now I grow so infirm that I'm bedridden, then I will ask someone to move my bed so that I can see the sunset. I will dance in partnership with the setting sun, letting it take the lead and I'll follow like a lady."

To Do or Not to Do

1. See the movie *Shall We Dance* (the original, not the J-Lo flick).
2. Hire a dance instructor and dare to glide gracefully.
3. Buy a twirly dress and dance to the pulse of each day's rhythm.
4. Share cake with a friend and confide in her what you're up to.
5. Write down all your brilliant observations and turn them into greeting cards.

"Somebody's birthday, dance; somebody has died, dance.
Somebody is ill, dance around him. Somebody is going for a journey,
give him a farewell dance. Somebody is coming,
welcome him with a dance. Make it a point that the more you
dance, the more you are in tune with God."

—Osho

Song Therapy

If you remember Elvis, the Beatles, or Carol King. If you know the lyrics to even one Simon and Garfunkel song. If you've ever hummed "I Can't Get No Satisfaction" in the shower. If you've swooned to the soft, slow melody of a saxophone. If Sting can take your breath away. If you remember the joy of singing with a busload of friends on the way to summer camp, but now you're too embarrassed to sing. If you think you can't carry a tune. If your heart is broken, if you're dealing with a loss, struggling with your looks, or wrestling with health issues, then you might benefit from singing therapy. If you remember ABBA. If you can relate to any of these ifs, you're definitely old enough to try singing.

If you've ever lost yourself in the fervor and delight of a drumbeat, you know that some emotions can't be spoken. Deep feelings are most exquisitely expressed through music and song.

Please don't say, "But I can't sing." Don't even go there. Singing is intuitive, it comes naturally. It's a right-brain thing, an unfettered spirit spilling forth. If you've ever listened to slow strings of a violin duet, you know the stirrings of joy and sadness that a soft melody elicits. If you've ever lost yourself in the fervor and delight of a drumbeat, you know that some emotions can't be spoken. Deep feelings are most exquisitely expressed through music and song.

"I sing better now than when I was younger," fifty-six-year-old Lisa says. "My voice is deeper and richer, not as thin. I like to sing. My voice has more resonance. It's not good, but I appreciate it." The other day Lisa caught herself singing and thought to herself, "That sounds damn good, I think I'll sing it again."

When we're singing, we're feeling rather than thinking. Try it, just sing along right now. Warm up! *La-la-la, do-re-me, do-re-me*. Here we go. Read the words and give it a tune, "Do your boobs hang down, do they jiggle to and fro, can you tie them in a knot, can you tie them in a bow?" See what I mean? Isn't it fun and don't you feel better already about sagging breasts? Yes, our boobs are hanging lower than they did ten years ago, but that doesn't mean we should stop singing. In fact, it is often through singing that despair turns into hope.

Irena started a singing group when her beloved husband, Joe, was diagnosed with bone cancer. Joe was once the lead singer in a weekend garage rock and roll band and a soloist for weddings and in the church choir, and he says, "Singing is my therapy." So when chemo and radiation began, Irena felt so helpless about his treatment that she didn't know what else to do but encourage her husband to sing. She put out fliers, invited neighbors, and passed the word among friends that she was having a sing-a-long on Saturday night. Four people came, there weren't any instruments, and the singing was all a cappella. For two hours they forgot all about the rigors of treatment. The group grew by word of mouth and soon a guitarist joined. Some people were shy at first, but as the weeks went by, everyone improved and the songs sounded better as more voices joined in.

Nothing could have prepared Irena and Joe for the exuberance and depth of emotion that singing with the shadow of death in the room brought. A sense of release and relief filled in the air as they held hands and sang together. Emotions that were too strong for words expressed themselves in song. Feelings that had been bottled up for weeks melted away with the music. Eleven months later, on a Sunday morning Joe died at home. The night before twenty-seven singers, a guitarist, and a flutist circled his bed and filled the room with soft vibrations and song.

To Do or Not to Do

1. Sing in the shower. If you still don't like the sound of your voice, ask a friend to take a shower and harmonize with you. Voices sound better in a group.

2. Pass on your songs. Teach your kids the songs you sang at summer camp and in your sorority days.

3. Chart the history of your life by the music you have listened to.

4. Learn to play chords on a guitar and make up a song about body parts.

5. Start a singing group. *Buy the book Rise Up Singing: The Group Singing Songbook* by Peter Blood (Independent Publishers Group, 1988). Invite the neighbors.

———

"Once upon a time, wasn't singing a part of everyday life?"
—Pete Seeger

Doing the Loop

Do you get lost when driving the car? Do you get north and south mixed up? Do you intend to go in one direction and end up going in another? By the time we reach middlescence, we have probably all done the loop many times. Jean and I are soul sisters, and we always do the loop to get to where we are going. We met on the first day of college over forty years ago, and since our first meeting on the third floor of our freshman dorm, we've been living on the edge. We may look innocent, but we can cut loose. No one ever suspected that we were the ones throwing the water balloons from the roof of Doney Hall.

We can talk about anything. Our take on love and politics, men and marriage, clothes and shopping, art and children, and what matters most has kept our friendship tight. When we reunited after ten years of being apart, it only took an evening of "what do you think about such and such?" to be reassured that we were still in sync. She favors Johnny Depp over Ben What's-his-name just like I do. She prefers independent film to blockbusters. She'd rather take the bus to town than drive, and she subscribes to *Gourmet* magazine, as do I.

Not only do we have magazines and bus trips in common, we also have identical flaws. For one thing, we're directionally impaired—we get turned around going where we're going. We know where we intend to go and eventually we get to where we're headed, it's just that we get there by going roundabout. Whenever Jean and I take a road trip together, first we fantasize about all the spots that we'd like to visit—the spa on Vancouver Island, the Shakespeare festival in Ashland, the Sea Lion Caves on the Oregon Coast. Once we decide on our destination, we look at the map, mark the most direct route, and head out. We give ourselves plenty of time for potty breaks, garden shops, and thrift stores. Since Jean is a maple bar gourmet, we brake for all doughnut shops. Our intention is to travel from point A to point B and reach our destination in time for martinis. With all that planning you'd think we could get to where we were going without much confusion, but honestly I can't think of one trip where we didn't get north and south discombobulated. No matter how familiar we are with the roads, we always do the loop. Even when we're cruising south on Highway 101 to spend the night at her beach house, the house she's driven to dozens of times, we either miss the turn-off or take the wrong exit. "The ocean on our right," she points and I can see it, and we head north when we should have gone south. If I dig in my purse to find my reading glasses and map, it's usually too late because by then fate is in charge of the itinerary.

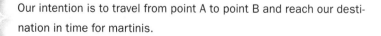

Our intention is to travel from point A to point B and reach our destination in time for martinis.

Like the time we almost missed our flight to meet our college sorority sister Virginia in California. Jean and I were visiting about such and such and hadn't noticed that we were sitting in the wrong waiting room, waiting for the wrong flight. That was the only time I remember Jean getting ruffled. Virginia had free passes to take us to Disneyland and neither of us wanted to miss that! Not to worry! The unseen forces work in mysterious ways. Jean noticed that there was no plane at the gate and that got my attention. "Hurry, Jean, hurry!" OK, so we were the last to board. What matters is that we didn't have to get a motel at the airport or lie to Jean's husband, George, about where we were. We cut it close, but we didn't lie.

That's what I enjoy about traveling with her—living on the edge. Even our hometown outings take about two to four hours longer because we get off track. We never think of it as getting lost though, we think of it as "doing the loop." "Oops, we're doing the loop," I'll say. "Yup," she'll nod, "I wonder how that happened?"

I'm sure you've done the loop and survived it too. By this age most of us have. Just when we think we're heading in one direction, we take the loop and end up someplace else.

Doing the loop doesn't phase Jean much. How could it? She's a cancer survivor. A little thing like getting lost is, for her, a good day. Doing the loop comes with surviving. I'm sure you've done the loop and survived it too. By this age most of us have. Just when we think we're heading in one direction, we take the loop and end up someplace else. I don't mean to sound morbid, but we all know that life's a journey with death as destination. "Thank heavens," Jean says, "that it's not a straight trip to get there." So here's to living on the edge and doing the loop. Here's to seeing the scenery and surviving.

To Do or Not to Do

1. Call your soul sister and ask her if she wants to take a road trip.
2. Check out the doughnut shops along the way and send the location of the one with the best maple bars to me. I'll pass the info on to Jean.
3. Don't call Virginia! She can't get any more free passes.
4. Live on the edge. Do the loop and when all else fails you can depend on yourself.
5. Carry reading glasses in case you need to read a map.

"Everything is so dangerous that nothing is really very frightening."

—Gertrude Stein

No More Desperate Housewives

Let's be honest. We midlife darlings have all had a few nervous break-downs. We have all been angry and hid it. We have all been depressed. We have all felt desperate at times. We may be able to do it all and have it all, but often the stakes are too high. In the process we forget what we really want, think, and feel.

"How did you treat housewife syndrome?" I asked her. "Oh, back then we just had nervous breakdowns," she laughed.

Though she's never seen the show, Margaret remembers feeling desperate at certain times in her marriage. In her day, they called it "housewife syndrome." She knew she had it because she was obsessed with cleaning the house. The carpet had to be vacuumed so the pile went all one way. No one was allowed to touch the towels hanging in the bathroom. "How did you treat housewife syndrome?" I asked her. "Oh, back then we just had nervous breakdowns," she laughed.

Margaret told me she was driven to be the ideal mother, wife, and hostess. She insisted that her husband not light the fire in the fireplace until the guests were walking up the stairs. She wanted everything to be timed perfectly. As he lit the match she'd put on a tape to the exact song she wanted playing as the guests walked in the room. If the fire and music didn't come together, she felt she was a failure.

Margaret was angry inside, but she didn't share that with anyone. She kept it in and became more depressed and anxious. She had a few panic attacks and crying jags. She felt gloomy inside, but she smiled and put on her happy face. When friends and family asked how it was going, she always said, "Fine."

We have all done this—we've all said "Fine" when we felt angry. We were taught that anger was an emotion to be squelched—it was not something that ladies expressed. Instead of speaking up we turned anger on ourselves and got depressed. What we didn't know then that we know now is that anger about a situation is a clue—it tells us something isn't right.

After her nervous breakdown, Margaret went to counseling, joined a women's group, and figured out that something wasn't wrong with her, but rather that something was wrong. She didn't like her home situation, and so she decided to start saying so. She became less desperate when she began speaking up. She has been speaking up for ten years now.

At middle age, we stop looking the other way. We speak up. If our relationships are unhealthy, if our jobs are demeaning, if our communities and schools are in crisis, we are saying so. We are not putting the "it's just fine" label on injustice anymore. It is not fine with us that children are neglected and abused. It is not fine with us that health care is so expensive. It is not fine with us that our young men and women are sent to war. It is not fine with us that our environment is suffering. It is not fine with us that funding for the arts has been cut. It is not fine with us that sex and violence is used to sell everything.

Watch out! Middle-agers are not depressed or desperate any more. We've been through therapy and read self-help books. We have worked hard and improved ourselves. We have been on our knees and prayed. We have asked for help and received it. We have opinions and we are letting our voices be heard.

To Do or Not to Do

1. Express yourself. Turn depression into expression and let your opinions and ideas be known.
2. Repeat after me: "I am a lovely woman even if I get angry."
3. Tell it like it is. If you feel a nervous breakdown coming on do not say, "Oh, I'm just fine."
4. Vacuum as much as you like, but let the family use the towels.
5. Hip, hip, hooray for every woman who is making a positive difference in her family, her community, and the world.

"When we were children, we used to think that when we were grown-up we would no longer be vulnerable. But to grow up is to accept vulnerability. To be alive is to be vulnerable."

—MADELEINE L'ENGLE

Reading Glasses, Comfy Shoes, and a Signature Look

A signature look is a must for a perimenopausal or a postmeno-pausal woman. Picking out your reading glasses, buying your com-fortable shoes, and designing your look can take your mind off all your symptoms.

Katharine Hepburn had a signature look and so does my friend Gethen. I wish you could see her. Picture this. Gethen is 5'7", a size 6, and she looks like a million bucks in whatever she wears. She wore a long pink silk chiffon straight skirt and a tight-fitting sheer jacket to match at her son's wedding and was drop-dead gorgeous. Everyone noticed. With all the compliments she received you'd think she'd con-sider wearing it more often, but she swears she'll never wear that outfit again. She isn't comfortable in form-fitting or clingy, that isn't her style. Gethen fancies loose and understated. She prefers monochromatic beige or tan, enormous sweatshirts, oversized sweaters, wide-legged pants, and long, flowing trench coats. That's it. Oh yes, and big, oval-shaped, tortoise-rimmed glasses. Whatever she buys, it has to be big. Imagine a perfectly ironed, light beige sweatshirt hanging gracefully over perfectly pressed, wide-legged beige wool pants. Not a wrinkle or a bulge showing. Imagine huge, round, tortoise-framed glasses and a hooded coat to the ankles. That's Gethen. That's her signature look. Classic supersized sweatshirt, timeless. She's the only woman I know who looks sophisticated wearing a triple size X purchased in the big men's department.

A signature look is a style that's different from merely being stylish. As young women, we liked hip. We went for trendy. We liked dressing to be noticed. As mature women, we often feel jarred by the percep-tion that we're no longer attractive. That's ridiculous! Let's put an end to that! Instead of dressing to knock *their* socks off, let's dress to knock *our very own* socks off. Then we'll really be appealing. Then when we walk into a room they'll notice not what we're wearing but how we're wearing it. We'll be gorgeous because we know who we are and we're flaunting it.

> As young women, we liked dressing to be noticed. Now, instead of dressing to knock their socks off, let's dress to knock *our very own* socks off.

Rachel also has a signature look. She's got gypsy spirit in her blood and that's the style she's going for: layered ruffled skirts, silver belts and bracelets, boots, hoop earrings, and mix-matched colors. Rachel's reading glasses—zebra, tiger, striped, or polka dot—hang around her neck on a jeweled chain.

Anna's signature look is black: chunky silver bracelets, diamond earrings, and small, black horn-rimmed glasses. Black for all occasions—pants, jackets, dresses, skirts, blouses, scarves, coats, purses, gloves, tights, and shoes. Anna has her signature shoes nailed down too—black and comfy. Comfy sandals, Mary Jane flats, and walkers.

It's taken us forty years or more to figure out who we are, and now that we know who we are, it's our civic duty to the women following in our footsteps to change the perception that we stop being attractive at thirty-five. Every woman has her own personality, and it's our moral obligation to make a powerful statement. That way young women will be encouraged by our courage. When it comes down to it there's so much in life that we can't control that we might as well take charge of what is within our influence. We can choose our eyeglasses, our shoes, and our clothes. Our signature look is a style of dressing that reflects our very own character; it expresses our artistic touch. A signature look is head to toe dressing—from eyeglasses to comfy shoes—that says, "I know who I am and your opinion of me is none of my business. My business is to be comfortable, look great, and be myself."

To Do or Not to Do

1. Choose reading glasses first. Take a friend along for consultation. Once you've figured out what style looks really good on your face, you'll be ready to plan your signature look around them. Buy five pair. You don't want to be caught reading wearing ugly ones.

2. Design your signature look by creating a wardrobe portfolio. Cut pictures of dresses, pants, and jackets from magazines. Arrange them artistically and paste them into the portfolio. This will be your reference point and shopping guide.

3. Choose your signature color. Are you black, monochromatic, or colorful?

4. Buy comfortable shoes. I personally like Taryn Rose (she was trained as an orthopedic surgeon). They're luxurious and comfy. Expensive, but worth it. The way I see it, you can't look good if your feet hurt.

5. Give away everything in your closet that you can't fit into, or that you don't like, or that you haven't worn in the last year. If it's vintage—that's more than twenty-five years old—pass it on to your daughter or open a vintage clothing store.

"If you don't have real live majorette boots at this stage of your life, it's your own damn fault. Quit whining and go out and get some!"
—JILL CONNER BROWNE, Sweet Potato Queen

Sweet Signs of Impending Joy . . .

> You have learned from experience that keeping quiet is always a clever thing to say.
> You value an open heart. You do what it takes to keep yours wide open.
> You are preparing for your death by living juicy.
> You never miss an opportunity to have fun with another person.
> When you are feeling down you know that this too will pass.

Dressing for Retirement

Retirement isn't what it used to be. If you're panicked about what you're going to wear now that you're not going to the office every day, don't be. Look at it as yet another fabulous way to reinvent yourself.

My sister-in-law Cathy has been through the transition of dressing for the office to dressing for retirement. She's become an expert at dressing for the occasion. If she's headed for the Sweet Grass Dude Ranch in Montana, where she goes for seven days every summer, she dresses like a cowgirl in Wrangler slim-fit jeans with a touch of Lycra stretch. A fresh shirt with pearlized snap buttons, a straw cowboy hat, a leather belt with a silver buckle, and black or tan boots. The bandana is color coordinated to match the shirt she's wearing. If she's attending Sunday morning services at the positive-thinking New Age church, she definitely wears hippie-style flowing dresses. For golf her costume is usually country club togs, but if she's feeling a little outrageous she'll switch to leopard capris.

She likes dressing up. Clothes are her passion. The event may not be as critical as what she wears to it. Her outfits are carefully chosen to match her mood, the season, and the ambiance. It's like being a little girl and playing dress-up.

For Cathy dressing to match her corporate bank position made going to work for thirty-some years bearable. Wearing navy blue Yves St. Laurent suits and Stuart Weitzman high heels was the festive part of being a loan officer. Add a dark red leather Kenneth Cole briefcase and she's on top of her game.

That was her only angst about retiring. She was going to miss those outfits. What would she wear? What would she do with the closet full of work uniforms? Sure, she was looking forward to babysitting her two grandkids once a week and she knows what to wear to do that—comfy jeans and washable T-shirts. "And always makeup," she says. "I want the little kids to remember their bammy in makeup." But what will she wear the rest of the week? On those mornings when she wakes up and doesn't have an occasion? How will she dress? Sloppy is not her style, baggy doesn't do it, and the same outfit every day would be boringly monotonous.

"My job was so critical for thirty-four years. I put so much energy into it, and two weeks after I retired, poof, it's gone," Cathy said. "I'm so glad that I didn't overwork more than I did or pay a higher price, but what will I do with my clothes?"

Transitions throw us all off kilter, and for the first weeks of retirement Cathy was out of whack! That must have been the motivation behind accepting a new position right away. She could wear Yves St. Laurent again! So when she was offered another high paying position, she negotiated to share it with her husband, Jerry, also a retired banker. Semiretirement seemed like an ideal solution. She could wear high heels on Monday, Tuesday, and a half day Thursday.

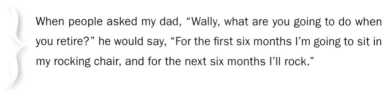

When people asked my dad, "Wally, what are you going to do when you retire?" he would say, "For the first six months I'm going to sit in my rocking chair, and for the next six months I'll rock."

We're all creatures of habit and old habits are hard to undo. Faced with the dilemma of what to do with her clothes, Cathy did the only thing she knew, and accepted a position in the very same field that she'd just left. It was flattering to be recruited and the big bucks were seductive, but she wasn't so sure. Was she merely repeating a career pattern? Was she choosing the same path again because it was the only way she knew to wear the clothes she'd collected? Was it possible to find a new avocation *and* a new style?

That's the dilemma. What to do in the gap, the space between one thing and another? What to do while passing through career into retirement? When people asked my dad, "Wally, what are you going to do when you retire?" he would say, "For the first six months I'm going to sit in my rocking chair, and for the next six months I'll rock." That's an enlightened perspective, don't you agree? Maybe the first six months of retirement is for sitting and the next six months is for rocking. With all that sitting and rocking you have space, for the first time in adulthood, to contemplate your next move and what you will wear.

Jerry decided he didn't want the job after all, so Cathy didn't take it either. It's been more than a year now since she's retired and she's happily mastering her clothes. For gardening it's a straw hat, special rubber gloves with a perfect fit, and slip-on green clogs. For painting the walls it's her white overalls. Oh! She looks darling in those!

To Do or Not to Do

1. For advice on dressing for the occasion, e-mail Cathy at *www. tootoochic.com* and tell her Judy sent you.

2. For advice on retirement, e-mail both Cathy and Jerry. They're the best-dressed money managers around.

3. Have a costume swap. Trade pieces of clothing and accessories that no longer suit you.

4. Sit in a rocking chair and contemplate your next career move, your next occasion, and what you'll wear.

5. Read *Love, Loss, and What I Wore* by Ilene Beckerman (Algonquin, 1995). It's a very stylish read!

"For the past few years, I have usually worn black.
Not because I'm sad but because dressing in black is always chic—
and makes shopping choices much easier. And also because
Audrey Hepburn wore black a lot and later so did Jackie."

—ILENE BECKERMAN

Ladies, Climb the Mountains

Hallelujah, we're in our prime! We've made it! We are over the hill. We have climbed the Decades Mountains. It was often quite difficult, but we did it and we're delighted to be in the second half. We have earned our wisdom and we are glad that experience shows. Oh sure, we have a few psychological dents from childhood, but for the most part we've straightened those out. In the big scheme of things, our quirks and imperfections are merely minor glitches that enhance our intrinsic womanly beauty and value.

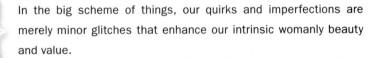

In the big scheme of things, our quirks and imperfections are merely minor glitches that enhance our intrinsic womanly beauty and value.

Marching through the twenties, we were scuffed up plenty, our egos were bruised. We made wrong turns, faced dead ends, got lost, recovered our equilibrium, and learned from our mistakes. It was not easy, but we admitted our errors, faced our demons, dusted ourselves off, and kept going.

Managing the thirties was tough. We were overwhelmed, straining to get everything to line up. We wanted it all—a relationship, a house, a picket fence, children, a career, a two-car garage. We expected ourselves to be perfect, and we tried our best to make it all perfect. It was daunting to keep it all in perfect order. We were frustrated, discouraged, and discombobulated. Some of us blew it. We felt crazy and out of whack. Our hearts were shattered. In the fog of failure and disappointment we sometimes went to bed, but we always got up. When we were exhausted from carrying too much heavy baggage, too many shoulds and wants and unrealistic expectations, we put one foot in front of the other and kept going. We managed to take care of so much. We took care of so many. How did we do it?

We've been climbing the youthful hills for four or more decades, and we've discovered that we're stronger than we thought we were. In some ways it is a shock to be older than we ever thought we would be. In the beginning we were young. Now we are in the middle. Older than we feel, older than we want to be, older than we think we are. It is painful at times to realize that we cannot go back. We went forward without knowing that we were. We accept where we are. We know that there are things we can control and much that we cannot. That is the understanding that comes with experience. It is not our looks or the things that we own, but our attitudes that shape us. It is the courage in our souls that defines who we are, what we can be, and where we go.

We have earned our "Over the Hill" birthday balloon. We have climbed dozens of mountains, we have been through dark nights, and we are still breathing. Whew! What an accomplishment! We are something! We are prime-timers.

So ladies, let's be proud of our wisdom. Yes, we have wrinkles and age spots, gray hair and middle-age spread, but we are not done, finished, or dried up. There are several dozen mountains ahead.

To Do or Not to Do

1. At your next birthday, buy yourself an "Over the Hill" balloon or button and wear it proudly. Don't fret about it being black—black is very chic.

2. Name the mountains that you've climbed. Examples: cranky, critical parent mountain, mean teacher mountain, sour romance mountain, childbirth mountain, carpool mountain, overdrawn checkbook mountain.

3. Say out loud, "What an accomplishment!"

4. Name the mountains that you want to climb. Examples: second career mountain, get the kids through college mountain, empty nest mountain, poetry class mountain, exotic travel mountain.

5. Hey prime-timers, start your engines, rev it up, pump up the power, and go.

"Being a recovering perfectionist myself, I have adopted as my motto
the disclaimer often found on clothes made of cotton or raw silk:
'This garment is made from 100 percent natural fibers.
Any irregularity or variation is not to be considered defective.
Imperfections enhance the beauty of the fabric.'"

—SUE PATTON THEOLE

Wiser Than Last Year

"I like wise women," forty-seven-year-old Marjie tells me. "I like hanging around them and listening to them. Someday I hope to be one." Women become wise not because we are innately smart, but because we have experience. We've made mistakes and gotten through. "Wise women have struggled like I have and they have come out of it," Marjie says. "Hearing their stories gives me confidence that I can survive too. I want my kids to think of me as a wise woman someday."

Some people freeze when they're afraid, but not Marjie. The more fearful she gets the faster she moves, the quicker she talks, and the broader she smiles. You can tell that she's upset because she talks in circles, trying to convince herself that she's all right. She smiles, talks, and moves all four limbs. She has so much nervous energy that if need be she might be able to heat up a room. "It keeps me thin," she says.

Marjie's husband left her broke and scared. "When you have teenage boys and not enough money, you're scared," she says, "and when you're forced to sell your home and move into a rented, broken-down cottage, you're scared." Marjie is accepting the challenge, though, raising her boys, talking to debtors, and going without. She doesn't know what tomorrow will bring, but she's taking it one hour at a time. That's what courage is, going into the unknown in spite of your fears. Marjie is putting aside her panic at being a single, middle-aged woman with two teenage sons and little money. She doesn't have much, but she's filling her home with laughter, kindness, and positive thoughts. She's doing what needs to be done for the sake of her children.

Marjie hangs out around wise women, and she's an A+ student. Whenever a wise woman talks, Marjie stops and takes notes so that she can rewrite what was said in her journal. "Can I borrow a pen?" she asks, "and a piece of paper?" Every week when I see her, she either says, "Judy, write that down," or "Judy, can I borrow a pen?" Then she asks, "Do you have any paper?" Once I wrote down, "Poor in money, rich in love" on a 3" × 5" notecard and Marjie took it home and hung it on her refrigerator. The next week she came back and said, "I like wisdom cards. Please write more wisdom down." Marjie may not come with pen or paper, but she always comes with an open heart. Marjie's transforming the breakdown of her marriage into a breakthrough for her soul.

The wisdom cards were a moment of reckoning for me. I didn't intend to become wise. It happened slowly, it sneaked up on me. I hadn't planned to say wise things, but I did and I amazed myself. There is a big responsibility with wisdom and, sadly, some women shrink from it—I knew I was at a crossroads. I could either claim the truth of who I had become or I could go into hiding and keep my true identity secret. I wish that I had had someone when I was younger—someone to offer advice, to point me in the right direction. Why would I refuse that honor? Why would I deny the younger women who might be in need of my guidance?

If we hide what we've been through, who will be there for the women following?

If we hide what we've been through, who will be there for the women following? Karolyn says she had a midlife crisis twice—one at thirty and one at forty. "I was afraid of being an adult," she says. It was wise women that she turned to. "I can't imagine what it would be like if we cut everyone off at fifty." We grow in wisdom, we don't attain it. Wisdom is the taste of our own experience. It's a deep understanding of what life is all about and of who we truly are.

To Do or Not to Do

1. Carry pens and paper so that when you're in the presence of a wise woman, you can take notes.
2. If you say something wise, write it down so that you will remember.
3. Decorate your home with laughter, kindness, and positive quotes.
4. Give a rose to a wise woman. Tell her that you appreciate her wisdom.
5. Accept that you are wise and be humble. We are wiser than last year, but we still have a way to go.

"The deepest experience of the creator is feminine,
for it is experience of receiving and bearing."
—RAINER MARIA RILKE

What Do You Want to Be When You Grow Up?

Remember when you were young and people asked you the question, "What do you want to be when you grow up?" It starts very young, sometimes as young as six or seven, and continues until we graduate from college or have gained a specialized skill. Then the questioning stops. It's been decided! You are who you are and that's it.

It's silly to ask a very young girl what she wants to be when she grows up. Childhood at its best is carefree. If we ask this of a young child, we are asking the wrong age group. We need to be asking this question of ourselves, again and again. With each decade we need to visualize who we want to be.

I ask myself, How do I want to spend my Goddess Years? What kind of person do I want to be in my 70s? Who do I want to be in my

80s? I know the Goddess Years are coming. Those years just around the bend when others will look to me to see what I am doing and how I am living. The world needs positive examples of women interested, interesting, and wise. That's why, when I'm feeling discombobulated, I might ask myself a couple times a day, "Judy, what do you want to be when you grow up?" That question keeps me focused on my goal. I want to be a Goddess. I want to be a woman worthy of admiration. I want to be a woman who honors her spiritual and human sides. I want to be a woman who is nurturing and compassionate toward the earth and all her creatures. I want to keep loving and learning. A Goddess knows that it is not how much love she receives, but how much love she gives. I want to have lots of fun and flirt. I want to be known as that old papier-mâché artist with a twinkle in her eye.

Right now I'm doing what I love—writing books, seeing clients, and making papier-mâché. I intend to continue doing all those things and add more. I'm more grown up than I used to be, yet I'm not fully developed. I want to explore kindness. I intend to keep working, but gentler. Not as frantically as I have in the past, but leisurely, for the joy of it all. I've got plans. I'd like to sell tickets at a movie theater, usher at the symphony, go back to school to study design, open up a cupcake bakery, and sell my papier-mâché bracelets and bowls at art fairs. I intend to flirt more, dance more, sing more, love more.

My seventy-seven-year-old friend Barbara is Goddess Dynamo. She plays tennis five times every week. We're talking singles here. She runs around the court faster than a youngster of fifty. Following tennis, she starts her business day. "I'm saving for retirement," she says. She represents a line of greeting cards and books. She oversees publicity for authors. And that's not all. She's an inventor. Her original lettuce keeper bag keeps greens fresher than any crisper or plastic bowl. She's the Queen of Motion. She calls on clients and drums up business. In the evening she cooks dinner for her eighty-two-year-old husband, Daryl, who is an entrepreneur. He designs, manufactures, and sells rabbit hutches, called rabbit condominiums. After dinner she goes for an hour-and-a-half trail ride on her bike. She is a role model of optimism.

Ask yourself, What do I want to be when I grow up? Write your answers down. Doesn't it seem increasingly clear that we must take our Goddess Years into our own hands if we want something exciting, creative, and precious to happen?

To Do or Not to Do

1. Ask yourself, What do I want to be doing when I grow up?
2. Remember you are a Goddess in Training. Ask yourself, How do I want to spend my Goddess Years? Ask yourself, What gives meaning to my life?
3. Be grateful for work. Work is a blessing. Get a job and do it gently.
4. Behave like a Goddess. Spread compassion and kindness. The world and all creatures need you.
5. Love more. Understand more. Flirt more. When in doubt about what is needed ask yourself, How would a Goddess respond?

"I always believed that whatever you are when you are young, as you age, you become more so."

—EVELYN LAUDER

Hooray for My Chocolate Coach

Why does it take decades for science to catch up with what women have always known? Chocolate is good for you. If women are craving chocolate, then that is an indication of a very sound reason behind it. I don't know why doctors are prescribing so many antidepressants and sleeping pills when they could be handing out chocolate instead. Women don't need science to prove that chocolate is a mood elevator and an aphrodisiac.

> Women don't need science to prove that chocolate is a mood elevator and an aphrodisiac.

With that in mind, I have set several healthy goals for the second half of my life, and I am in training to achieve them. My long-term goal is to incorporate a reasonable amount of dark chocolate into my diet. I have hired a coach to motivate and guide me. I am working toward making chocolate, along with fruits and vegetables, a staple in my pantry. My first objective is to learn how to get an unopened box of chocolate truffles safely home. They say that confession is good for the soul, and I must confess that I have opened a box of chocolates and eaten them all on the drive home. I don't want to do that anymore. My goal is to bring the box of truffles into the house and not eat them all within the first hour. I want to keep a box in my cupboard and eat only one piece per day just like Scarlet does. Scarlet is my chocolate coach.

Scarlet is a nutritional expert. She's been studying healthy living for five decades. She says dark chocolate is high in magnesium, which is good in alleviating mood swings. According to Scarlet dark chocolate is full of antioxidants. Antioxidants counteract destructive molecules, called free radicals, which may cause heart disease, cancer, and other ailments. Eaten in moderation dark chocolate has been found to lower blood pressure, inhibit bacterial buildup and plaque, increase energy, and calm the nerves.

According to Scarlet what women need are little truffles containing a minimum of 70 percent cocoa. That's the best way, she says, to satisfy a craving without consuming too much sugar and saturated fat.

We used to believe that illness was something over which we had no control. If we were sick there was no choice but to put ourselves in the hands of doctors. We now know that we have more control over our health and healing than we previously thought. As women, we must take charge of our own health maintenance, and that is why we should follow Scarlet's lead and eat more chocolate!

In the middle of the day Scarlet takes an hour to herself and consumes one piece of very fine dark chocolate. She also drinks one cup of black tea. Black tea, which contains catechins, has for years been considered a way to improve longevity. Scarlet swears by her daily ritual. It is as much a part of her healthy lifestyle as aerobics and stretching.

She never skimps on the quality of the chocolate. Only eat and drink the best, she says. Scarlet advises never to eat chocolate while walking, standing, or talking. It is of the utmost importance to sit down and pay attention—to make it part of a midday meditation.

I think she is right, and I'm doing my best to follow her excellent coaching. Moderation is Scarlet's trick. If we consume in moderation, we won't feel deprived. We won't fall victim to stuffing ourselves with cheap imitations because, on the cellular level, our bodies will know that we are treating them well. If we can be mindful for a few minutes each day of the rich flavor and smooth texture, we won't eat more than we need.

I am in phase one of my personal program. Once each day I sit down, eat my carefully chosen truffle, and drink a cup of black tea. When I am done I telephone my coach and report the progress. I have that portion of the program down perfectly. I have never skipped a day. There are other aspects of the program, however, where I am stuck. I have not mastered having truffles in my cupboard. I am still working on not eating the entire box. For some reason I feel compelled to eat any chocolate within reaching distance; therefore, I have a problem keeping truffles from one day to the next.

I am a difficult case, so Scarlet is taking emergency measures on my behalf. Since I can't be trusted with an entire box, she is going to deliver one chocolate per day to my home. If she is not available, then I have agreed to go out, buy one chocolate, and take it to a coffee shop and order tea. I have promised to eat it there. She says that when I have mastered this for six months I will be reprogrammed. My unconscious will know that chocolate is always available. When that happens I will be ready to bring a pound into my home.

I am encouraged that in the second half of my life I will be able to achieve my goal. The other evening I called my eighty-three-year-old mother. She said she was craving dessert. I asked her if she would like me to bring something over. "Well, I still have all these chocolates left from Christmas," she said. "Why don't you eat one of those?" I asked. "Oh, I don't think so," she said, "I'm saving those in case someone drops over for tea." That gives me hope that I, too, will have inherited this ability. In the second half of life I am confident that I can conquer my chocolate compulsion, bring boxes home with me—unwrapped—enjoy the pleasure of just one per day, and leave the rest in case someone drops over. And I'm counting on my chocolate coach to see me through the process.

To Do or Not to Do

1. Get a chocolate coach. Meet with her daily for chocolate reprogramming and motivation.

2. Alleviate chocolate guilt by confessing your chocolate sins. If we get it off our chest it might not stick on our thighs.

3. Drink a cup of tea and consume one truffle every day for six months. After that consider making chocolate a staple in your pantry.

4. Sit down. Never talk, stand, walk, or read while eating chocolate.

5. Be mindful when chocolate is within reaching distance. Choose only the best dark piece, sit quietly, close your eyes, and focus on the flavor and texture.

*"Strength is the capacity to break a chocolate bar into four pieces
with your bare hands—and then eat just one of the pieces."*

—Judith Viorst

Once in Your Lifetime

A week before Amanda moved out of our home in the suburbs to an apartment in the city, she crawled into my bed and we reminisced about mother-daughter transitions. "Mom," she pleaded out of the blue, "I don't want you to die." "Oh, honey," I said, "I'm not planning to check out anytime soon." Packing her stuff and moving out of her room must have triggered thoughts of death and separation. "You know what, Manda?" I said, "If I'm dead and you're alive, be happy for me. I got my wish. My prayer is to die before you." That is what all parents want; we hope to die before our children do. "Even though we will be apart," I told her, "we are always united through our love." We talked about her apartment and I cried about that.

"I've been a mother for so long," I said, feeling sorry for myself, "I won't know what to do without you around the house."

"Mom, don't be silly," she reassured me. "You can call or come visit." "But," I asked her, "what will I do with myself the rest of the time?"

"Mom," she advised, "make a list of the wild things that you would like to do just once."

Amanda moved out four years ago and I still cannot think of any wild things that I'd like to do that I haven't done. Except for spending a week at one of those gourmet meal spas, my desires are small. I do fantasize about selling my papier-mâché bracelets at an art fair. I do dream about hitting all the coffee shops around town. I picture myself sitting in the corner writing on my laptop. I'd like to have the persona of a real writer. The one thing that I actually do intend to plan is a Judy Is Out of Her Body party. (I've already been out of my mind.) I will leave instructions in the safety deposit box. I will burn a CD of the right songs to be played—songs that are important to me. I need to remember to leave the recipes for cupcakes and martinis to serve the guests.

My play-at-working attitude frees my mind for original thinking. Instead of doing what I have to do, I do what I'm inspired to do.

Even though there aren't any wild things that I want to do, there are activities that lend themselves to keeping us creative types spry. To get ideas, I sometimes ask other women, "What are the things that you would like to do at least once in your lifetime?" Hearing other women's responses gives me possibilities. Zoey, a teacher and part owner of a paint-on-pottery store recommends that every woman walk the labyrinth. The labyrinth, a metaphor for the journey of life, is a walking meditation. Lucy, a personal trainer, wants to play fairy godmother to an unsuspecting, underprivileged child. Margaret, a real-estate agent, would like to own a flower cart on the corner of Lake Washington Boulevard.

I make mental notes about the wild things I could do, but that doesn't mean I'll do them. I have been known to write long to-do lists, and once upon a time I followed them closely. As I checked the completed items off, I felt a wave of accomplishment. Perhaps it was my puritan work ethic that made me rather compulsive about getting things done. It was work first, play never. When Amanda moved out, I had a midlife awakening. Who was I if I wasn't a mother? Suddenly, my role was changing. Did I have to work so hard? Maybe I could play instead of working? I reevaluated my work addiction and developed a more relaxed philosophy. I'd rather play at working than work at working.

Following that principle, I adjusted my priorities and developed a more enlightened work ethic. I retitled my list "To Do or Not to Do." That way if I want to do what's on the list, I can, but if I change my mind and go in another direction, that's perfectly acceptable too. Now I am more apt to whistle while I'm working than grumble. My play-at-working attitude frees my mind for original thinking. Instead of doing what I have to do, I do what I'm inspired to do. I follow my own rhythm and I try to keep it lively. I make things up.

By the way, my sister-in-law Cathy says that when you get to the end of your to-do list it's over for you too. That's why I make sure that my mental lists are always very long.

To Do or Not to Do

1. Make a list of the wild things that you want to do at least once in your lifetime.

2. Take a pilgrimage to Notre Dame Cathedral at Chartres. Walk the labyrinth.
3. Give a tea party. Call it "Tea and Sympathy." Serve little sandwiches and big cookies, and share the joys and sorrows about the kids moving out.
4. Take a hiking vacation. Spend a week at a gourmet spa.
5. Write down the instructions for your "out of body" celebration. Hire the caterer. Throw it for yourself when you are good and ready.

"Life is a great big canvas and
you should throw all the paint on it you can."

—DANNY KAYE

The Essence of a Woman

I appreciate the Japanese aesthetic of wabi sabi. The essence of wabi sabi is that true beauty, whether it comes from an object, architecture, or visual art, doesn't reveal itself until the winds of time have had their say. A cracked pot, for example, has a quality that a perfectly formed pot is lacking. Beauty is found in the cracks, the worn spots, and the imperfect lines. Wabi sabi is the splendor of things modest and humble, the charm of things unique. To me, the essence of a woman's beauty is in the softening that experience brings.

Timeless beauty, like an etched patina, evolves over years, arriving slowly with the wear and tear of loving and being human. Such a woman retains the optimism of youth blended with compassion of forgiveness. She's strong yet fragile. She's pushed through difficult times and survived emotional storms. Endurance is written on her hands and face. She's learned that the secret of having it all is loving it all.

The beauty of a woman is that she can find the tiniest blessing even in the midst of heartache and growing older. When we get to be a certain age—the exact age is different for everyone—we begin to think a whole lot about aging. We begin to notice our hands, that the skin has grown thinner. We ask ourselves, What's that about? We start thinking about dying, crumbling, and fading away. A beautiful woman accepts those moments. She doesn't fight her despair. She embraces it and turns it around.

"Guess what?" Lee wrote to me. "I recently painted my floor red! I ripped up all of the old, dingy, formerly white turned to grayish carpet, used a whole can of putty to even out the raggedly wooden floor, and painted the whole thing a glorious color called Drumbeat. I love it so much. But I didn't paint the walls red; I painted them a pale peachy color, with all of the clarity of off-white, but just enough peach to give a warmth. Kind of like a vanilla yogurt, peaches and cream color. The combo is exquisite."

 Celebrating it all is what defines us. That's the spirit of a wabi sabi woman.

The more we celebrate being alive and all that means the better able we will be to say goodbye. Living is the preparation for parting. Celebrating it all, including broken pots and messed up canvas, is what defines us. That's the spirit of a wabi sabi woman. Everything is beautiful at its moment and every moment is passing. The closer things get to disappearing, the more exquisite they become. If you wake up in the morning and have the choice between mopping the floor and going for a walk, go for a walk. When you return you'll be energized by the freshness of the dew and ready to mop, yank up the carpet, *and* paint the floor. You'll be ready to paint the walls and your fingernails. You'll be alive and covered in paint.

To Do or Not to Do

1. Walk first. Mop the floor when you come home.
2. Cherish your individuality. Make your mark.
3. See beauty in everything. See beauty in yourself. It is a beautiful day.
4. Pause and reflect on the beauty of imperfection and impermanence.
5. Slow down, look closely, be patient. It's a wonderful world; take it in.

"I found God in myself and I loved her. I loved her fiercely."

—NTOZAKE SHANGE

Sweet Signs of Wisdom . . .

> Increasingly aware that you are closer to the end of your life than to the beginning, you wake up every day in awe.
> Increasingly aware that we are all spiritually connected, you would rather build a bridge than construct a wall.
> Increasingly aware that life is filled with absurdity, paradox, and riddles, you have stopped taking yourself seriously.
> Increasingly aware that fitting in is tiring, you allow yourself to rest and be amused.